POCONO GHOSTS,
LEGENDS AND LORE

DAVID J. SEIBOLD &
CHARLES J. ADAMS III

POCONO GHOSTS
Legends and Lore

Copyright 1991

All rights reserved. No portion of this book may be reproduced without written permission from the authors.

For information, write:
EXETER HOUSE BOOKS
P.O. Box 8134
Reading, Pa. 19601

PRINTED IN THE UNITED STATES OF AMERICA

CONTENTS

INTRODUCTION

I approached the researching and writing of a ghost book on the Poconos with a certain level of trepidation.

Under my literary belt (thin as it may be) were three volumes of ghost stories in Berks County, Pennsylvania; Cape May and Long Beach Island, New Jersey and the Delaware coast.

The Poconos were populated with resort hotels, time-shares and tourist traps, condos and concessions, and nothing more.

I needed some intensive re-education about a land I had at once over- and under-estimated.

I had over-estimated the crass commercialism of the region. This is mostly a veneer which may be a gleaming facade for those who choose to look no deeper. But beneath it is the rich grain of a fine stock.

My under-estimation of the Poconos was that it was probably devoid of any substantive legends and lore, and the ghosts which were abundant in the Pennsylvania Dutch Country and along the dunes and pine barrens of the Jersey Shore could certainly not exist in the Poconos.

Wow, was I wrong! After all, these now-romantic images of the windswept shore and placid Dutch Country villages, fields and forests were only made possible after the gaudy, glitzy and sometimes gauche realities of resort towns, boardwalks, honky-tonk amusement parks, pizza and tee-shirt shops and tourist traps in those locations were stripped away.

Estimations aside, I was more ignorant than anything else when it came to the heritage of the Pocono Mountain region.

This depth of character became more and more evident as I pored over ancient books, articles and newspaper accounts in historical societies and libraries. It also became evident that the publication of this book may well fill a void in contemporary writings on life beyond the timeshares and ski slopes of the Poconos.

This book does not intend to masquerade as a history book. Great pains have been taken to document and verify all stories, and every effort has been made to ensure accuracy in any and all historical accounts.

What is interesting about a book such as this is that legends and folklore become more pliable as the years go on. What happened to whom, and where it happened become vague clouds of fact that dissipate in the breezes of time and retelling.

Still, the stories endure, and endear themselves to generation after generation. Historians record the times, dates, places and names of their exacting discipline, and folklorists categorize and characterize the songs, stories and traditions of society. This volume is but another ear and another whisper down the alley.

Do ghosts exist? Who can say for certain? Do I believe in ghosts? How can I say for certain?

Does the little old lady in Stroudsburg, the one who sees her husband come back from the dead and visit her in her living room, believe in ghosts?

She tells her story through quivering lips and tearful eyes. Her beloved husband, three years in his grave, appears on no particular pattern in her living room as a misty form. He gets her attention with a slight wave of his hand and spends a few magical moments with her, silently communicating through time, space and reason.

To that woman, that figure is not a ghost, but a husband. To a hunter of and writer about the supernatural, of course, it is very much a ghost.

But it is a ghostly image and circumstance repeated

time after time and place after place to the point that to ask that woman and many like her if ghosts exist would be folly.

The wealth of folklore and the generosity and kindness of those willing to share their stories of ghostly encounters in the Pocono Mountains resulted in a slight change of our plans as we continued in the early stages of investigations and research.

What you are about to read is only a portion of the stories which have been accumulated in more than a year of intensive research. Several more tales, lacking either in details, verification or geographic relevance, fill our files and are likely to represent the basis for "Pocono Ghosts, Legends and Lore, Book Two" in the very near future.

Undoubtely the most pleasant thing to come out of our research for this volume was the friendliness, helpfulness and sincerity of the people we met along the way.

People like Harold Reedmiller, who at 87 had a rapier wit and ironclad recollection as he spun tales of his own childhood "haunted" place.

Later in life, Harold helped build places like the Tamiment lodge. When asked about any ghosts there, he scoffed, "Not that I know of. I guess when they saw me coming, they all ran away."

But it was another spot at another time in Harold's life that made him run and cower in childhood fear.

The Clay Hole, they called it. Along Creek Road, just off Route 209 above Marshalls Creek, this mysterious old swamp echoed with the sounds of an unearthly world. Distant forms and phantoms danced atop the rancid waters and scared the bejeebers out of local lads and lasses, Harold told us.

It was a neighbor lady called "Liz Jim" who started the rumors that ghosts and goblins infested the Clay Hole, and kids thereabouts were quick to test the hole and their own nerves.

Of course, the deep, gutteral, bone-chilling growls that rose from the swamp were nothing but the belches of bullfrogs.

The wispy figures that danced between the rotting trees were the product of foxfire and swamp gas.

But even with that knowledge, and many years of wisdom to temper it, the Clay Hole remains a foreboding place.

There are many places in the Poconos which harbor their secrets, lost in time.

Why and how, for example, Devil's Hole got its name remains a mystery.

Oddly enough, much of Devil's Hole, the creek, the road and the narrow ravine, is located in Paradise Township, Monroe County.

Some say the ruins of a building along one stretch of the crude creekside trail was a Prohibition-era speakeasy with its own stories locked in its crumbling stones.

And while nobody seems certain, Devils's Hole received its ominous name from an event which befits its bizarre monicker.

Today, Devil's Hole Road is a twisting, shady way which traverses quiet landscapes of field and forest, with lovely old estates and houses of newer construction dotting its sides.

But there is a recurring legend that trappers who settled in the area from their native France, met a bloody end when they were surprised by Indians along the creek. Depending on the source and version of the legend, the hapless Frenchmen were either hanged or butchered by the Indians as they tried to protect their land and their livelihoods from the intruders.

Frenchmen played a role in another legend near Canadensis. Deep in the woods there are the towering ruins of what is said to have been the beginnings of a castle, being hastily built as a possible refuge for an exiled French Queen Marie Antoinette. Of course, it is well known that the actual place carved out of the Pennsylvania forests which would have provided safe haven for the queen was what has become known as "Azilum," near Towanda in Bradford County.

But who knows? Perhaps the crude stone walls in that

Monroe County woods may, too, have indeed been constructed to possibly harbor the embattled queen. It is the stuff of legend, and in the Poconos, nearly every waterfall, swamp, river bank and mountain seems to have a story attached to it.

The Pocono Mountains, which were firmly established in the twentieth century as a four-season resort and recreation playground, were once undulating mounds beneath an inland sea.

Indeed, limestone outcroppings in Monroe and Carbon counties have been called Pennsylvania's Coral Reefs by geologists who marvel in the bounty of fossils that were imbedded in the rocks hundreds of millions of years ago when those rocks were shoreline.

Big Pocono Mountain, which at 2,100 feet above today's sea level is not tall in mountain terms, was tall enough to have stood above the glaciers of the ice age.

The ancient geological history of the region is complex and a marvelous study, but it is the history of those who have populated the Poconos that provide even more fascinating tales.

Natives, now known as Lenni Lenape, lived here more than 8,000 years before the birth of Christ. It is presumed they called the region Minisink. Some researchers believe the people called themselves Munsees, or the "People of the Rock Country."

Indian villages dotted the hills and valleys on both sides of the Delaware River, and even on islands in the stream.

The Poconos remained isolated while settlements grew into villages, villages into towns and towns into cities to the east and south. When a road was finally cut from Easton to Stroudsburg in the 1770s, growth came quickly to the remote mountains.

A second growth spurt came in 1853, when the Delaware, Lackawanna and Western Railroad brought investors, developers, industrialists and those who sought the clean air and peace the Poconos offered.

Along with that growth came the native customs and,

yes, superstitions of the settlers, and life in the land of the People of the Rock Country changed forever.

It is from Native Americans that some of the most powerful legends have been handed down. While most fit into the motifs of Indian tales which are indigenous to most areas where eastern Indians once lived, some are rather unique.

Just over the river from Pennsylvania, on Blackhead Mountain, some in New Jersey say there was a dead pine tree which stood on a ledge which was long favored by young couples seeking a quiet and remote spot for their amorous adventures.

It is said that the old tree, if trees could talk, would have many a story to tell. In fact, legend has it that the tree is inhabited by the spirit or spirits of one particular couple who romantic intensity was such that the old pine, very much alive when they began their mountainside tryst, withered, died and burst into flame under the lovers heat.

In his 1870 book, "Delaware Water Gap," Luke W. Brodhead affirmed that "vague and uncertain sounds are heard to issue from the place even on moonlight evenings, in tones from a gentle whisper to plaintive lamentations."

Indian legends are bountiful along the Delaware River, and particularly at the Delaware Water Gap.

The gap was the first place to feel the rush of the resort crowd. Antoine Dutot started construction on the massive Kittatinny House in 1829 and Samuel Snyder completed it years later. As the railroad brought the vacationers, more resorts rose at the gap and throughout the hills.

Dutot, who came to Pennsylvania from Santo Domingo after a slave revolt there in 1793, had actually envisioned and planned a major city for the Water Gap, but could not find the support for his dreams.

In some ways, and with due respect to the people, craft and specialty shops, restaurants, and the surviving hotels of Delaware Water Gap, the town is itself a ghost. It is certainly a ghost of what it might have been and was when its hilly streets and the roads which led from them were alive with those who sought relief from the demands of their city existence.

Now, the town is a pleasant place, severed from the main thruways, but still the site of a fine museum, excellent shopping and dining, and quiet quaintness.

Fueled by rushing streams, tumbling waterfalls and icy springs, the Delaware surges in an eternal swath between the hulks of Mt. Minsi on the Pennsylvania side and Mt. Tammany in New Jersey. The roar of its rapids has been challenged by the steady whir of traffic on the interstate highway, but that incessant rumble seems mute as the rising or setting sun angles its light around the rugged shoulders of sharp rocks and soft treetops.

The two mountains which are split by the river owe their modern names to their first human residents.

Minsi is derived from the tribal name, and Tammany comes from Chief Tamaneno. Interestingly, Tammany also lent its name to the notorious New York political society once ruled by the infamous Boss Tweed.

Several ancient skeletons which are believed to have been those of Indians, have been found on the slopes of the hills there, and those hills are also haunted by the restless spirits of at least two young Indians.

On a precipice near the site of the old Kittatinny Hotel is Lovers Leap, where the ghost of one sorrowful Indian lover can be detected.

The name, Winona, is familiar for its many attachments in the Poconos, and in the Water Gap area is where, according to tradition, the Indian princess by that name met her fate.

Winona was the beautiful and brilliant daughter of Wissinoming, the powerful Lenni Lenape chief.

When Dutch explorers ventured into the Pocono Mountains from their settlements along the Hudson River, Winona quickly befriended many of them, especially one Hendrick van Allen, a keen hunter and visionary. He saw minerals and mines in the hills, and pursued his visions with vigor.

As long as the peaceable Chief Wissinoming was alive, all went well between the whites and the natives. But when Winona's father finally passed away, the fears of his people that less placid tribes may opt to wage war on the Dutch and disrupt the tranquility of the mountains.

Indeed, those more hostile tribes betrayed Wissinoming's desires and began attacks on whites. Winona watched in fear and revulsion as many of her Dutch and Indian friends fell victim to each others' aggressions.

Winona tended to assimilate with the whites, and even chose to live in their village. Eventually, she spent much time paddling her canoe around the islands of the Delaware River and struck up a close relationship with van Allen. He taught her the ways of the Europeans and she eventually managed to learn those ways while not totally compromising her Indian upbringing.

Eventually, the British took over the land interests from the Dutch and van Allen was ordered by Dutch officials to abandon the mines he established and return to Holland. He was saddened, and when Winonna found out, she was devastated.

One night before she found out, however, she asked her friend to meet her at a spot where the Analomink Creek and Delaware River meet, downstream from her village.

At the point of their rendezvous, she had no knowledge of the news van Allen was about to reveal. She arrived with a spirit lightened at the prospect of meeting the man who apparently had won her heart.

Instead, van Allen showed her the letter form his Dutch superiors. Winona reacted stoically. Hardened by the deaths of those around her and the uncertainty of the times since the passing of her father, she decided her fate instantly.

These words are attributed to Winona as she spoke to van Allen:

"Winona will not stay to stem the current alone. The Great Spirit who rules the heaven is the father of Winona's people. He calls Winona home. Farewell, brother, tutor, lover; Winona's sun has set forever."

With that, she bolted fom van Allen's open arms to a cliff and to her death.

The Dutchman ran in pursuit and in desperation caught her at the edge of the rocky height. They embraced one last time, and in their euphoria they lost their balance and tumbled to their deaths.

To this day, this horrid leap of death is played out at the Delaware Water Gap in the form of fire lights which plummet down the cliff near the river.

The energy of Winona and van Allen becomes visible on misty evenings on the cliff of death.

To many Pocono residents, these Indian legends take on more profound proportions when they translate into frightening experiences they simply cannot fathom.

Take, for example, the happenings inside a home along Sherwood Forest Road near Neola.

Stan Romansky may have stirred the spirit of at least one Indian when he made some modifications in his home.

"I never believed any of this stuff until it happened to me," he said. And while nothing of monumental consequences took place in his home, what did happen would be enough to frighten even the bravest mortal.

Stan had to make some structural changes in his home to accommodate a new spiral staircase he wanted to install.

Little did he realize, but when he made those changes, he also unleashed what one respected medium told him was the spirit of an Indian.

Soon after the initial renovations began, strange things started to happen in the house in which life had been tranquil and uneventful up to that time.

Stan's brother witnessed a door open and close on its own. Stan's former wife detected an icy chill in certain spots in the house.

The most bizarre episode to take place there, however, was what Stan described as the ghostly figure of what he believed to be an Indian. It appeared as a cloudly blur, standing very near the spot where Stan had made room for the spiral staircase.

His ex-wife's mother had been in contact with the New York medium, and called her in to investigate the phenomena.

The medium "read" the house and confirmed that the restless energy of an Indian had been shaken loose by Stan's construction.

After some incantation and a ritual of exorcism, the medium left the place.

So did, says Stan Romansky, the icy chills, the sounds and the apparition of the Indian.

This story is a sampling of what you are about to read in Pocono Ghosts, Legends and Lore.

As the mountains have borne their share of true ghost stories from real people, they have also given up their share of tall tales.

The Indians had their Mesingw, the smelly, cantankerous spirit of the forest which kept hunters and children in line. Mesingw roamed the forests and possessed supernatural powers. Ceremonies to honor Mesingw were held and dolls in its image were crafted as men donned beaver robes, wooden or bark masks and danced so that the fickle forest beasts would bless their hunting and planting.

The early settlers had their own tales of mysterious creatures, as well. Around Peck's Pond, some folks still recall the stirring accounts of black snakes the size of logs, and some which could and did swallow each other. Around there, too, were fifteen feet-long hoop snakes, which rolled down hills with its tail in its mouth until it would unfurl to strike and sting any intruders with its poisonous tail.

A mysterious creature has been reported in the Water Gap area, according to several reports which have been investigated over the years by Stroudsburg researcher and photographer Chip Decker.

Decker refers to the elusive being as the Delaware Water Gap Hooter, and several persons have reported an unfamiliar sense of pressure, eeries stillness and odd hooting noises in the brush at the gap. Experienced birders and naturalists who have heard the hooting cannot associate it with any known bird or animal, and say it is not from a human voice.

These are but a few examples of the ghost stories, legends and lore of the Poconos. What follows are the stories, many in the words of those who lived them, which represent the pith and the grain of the solid stock that is Pennsylvania's Poconos.

From the sturdy trunk of the Poconos' heritage tree extend many branches. And, to be honest, in it are some knotholes. Those nubby aberrations have been taken into consideration, but we have chosen to seek the brilliant foliage of folklore to present in this volume.

We hope you enjoy it.

Charles J. Adams III
David J. Seibold
Marshalls Creek, Pa.
April, 1991

THE PHANTOM HOUSEMOTHER

They call her Mrs. Booth. "As long as anyone can remember, Mrs. Booth has been a part of Phi Sigma," says one fraternity brother.

She is a being whose mortal realities have been lost in time. But to many of the young men who have passed through Phi Sigma, her spirit remains very much intact within the walls of their beloved house at 91 Analomink Street in East Stroudsburg.

In fact, the story goes that Mrs. Booth herself, in a very literal way, indeed does remain within the walls of the stately Victorian mansion.

"Her ashes are buried in one of our fireplaces," says one who purports to know the story as well as anyone.

Nobody's quite certain in which of the several fireplaces her ashes are ensconsed, although some residents claim they can detect the location based on the supernatural activity which seems to swirl around one particular hearth.

This invisible matron in Phi Sigma is elusive, as spirits go, but her legend has passed through several generatons of frat house denizens. One man says, "She's been seen, supposedly, by two brothers I know of, one of which was in our time, about 1989.

"He said he saw a lady in a dress. He was all by himself at the time, and he wasn't under the influence of anything, if you know what I mean."

Yes, sir, we know what you mean. It is easy to conceive of old Mrs. Booth as just another concoction from the overactive imagination of upperclassmen. Nearly every college and university everywhere seems to have its ghostly legends. Dorms, libraries, "old mains" and quadrangles in institutes of higher learning across the world are awash with tawdry, titillating tales of suicides, murders and bizarre deaths of all fashion which have led to time-worn tales of terror on campus. East Stroudsburg University, and its associated frat houses and off-campus residences, have their share of these stories, as well.

While some of these stories may have bases in fact and strong legendary legs to stand on, others can be dismissed as the products of mild hysteria or hyperbole. Both ghost story researchers and readers must let each story stand on its own merit.

As for Mrs. Booth, her ghostly form has been seen and her ethereal energy felt throughout the frat house. "One of the guys," says one frat spokesman who declined to be identified, "saw the figure of a ghostly woman on the top floor. It was dark, night time, and he described it as the glowing image of a woman. That's all I can tell you."

Another brother reported an out-of-body experience and episodes of dizzying, stifling fear and confusion. He blamed Mrs. Booth for the irrational and uncharacteristic behavior.

Mrs. Booth is believed to have been a former owner of the old house at 91 Analomink, and while those who share that residence with her ghost claim she has created incidents of minor havoc, they do not fear her presence.

As our informant freely admits, "One of the brothers did tell me that he definitely saw the face of a woman staring at him one time on the second floor. She seemed to smile at him, as if she meant no harm."

"He said he smiled back at her, and the face slowly vanished."

While Mrs. Booth may continue to make her presence felt in that fraternity house, another wispy, womanly wraith torments another house just up the street, as we shall learn in the next chapter.

BEWARE OF BEATTIE!

Starting college can be disconcerting, even without the prospect of sharing your apartment with a ghost staring you in the face.

The home at 151 Analomink Street in East Stroudsburg is typical of the handsome dwellings along that tree-shaded street just off campus. Expended as a private residence, the two-story frame building has, in recent years, become the boarding house for a succession of East Stroudsburg University students.

It is also, if reports are to be believed, the permanent residence of a harmless but hapless spirit who has come to be known as "Beattie."

How the name came to be attached to the wraith is not clear, and perhaps as lost in legend as the origin and veracity of the stories which have been passed down over the years by those who have spent time in the old home.

As ghostly regions go, the home is in the thick of things. Elsewhere in this volume you will read of the spirits inside the fraternity houses of Phi Sigma Kappa (just down the street) and Sigma Pi (just up the street).

Analomink Street itself has all the trappings which are generally associated with hauntings. Craggy trees and Victorian turrets draw attention above eye level, and nearly every old home would seem to have its tale of human drama and, perhaps, the supernatural.

The shady way extends from the quaint old railroad station-turned-restaurant Dansbury Depot and Crystal

Street to the summit of a hill on which Sigma Pi sits on a broad expanse along Smith Street.

Back at 151 Analomink, the ghost of "Beattie" can be traced to at least several years ago, when strange happenings began to be noticed in the second floor rooms, staircases and attic of the home.

Imagine, if you will, arriving at the apartment which will be where you will study, sleep, party and ponder, and being told, in a matter-of-fact tone, "Don't be afraid if you see something. The ghost of a woman has been seen in this place a few times."

Nice thought, eh?

That is exactly the greeting a group of young coeds received when they moved into the Analomink Street house a few years back. Neighbors, former residents and classmates all had heard the stories, and while they generally paid them little mind and saw little reason for real concern, they did treat the reports of ghostly activity in the building with respect.

Our first contact with someone who had heard the tales was with the mother of an E.S.U. student who was moving into the house and called "mom" with the news of her alleged unseen roommate.

"My daughter mentioned it to me," the mother said, "and I told her just to watch out for whatever might happen."

The mother was tolerant, and, in fact, a believer in the supernatural world which exists beyond the understanding of most people.

After a short time in the house, the mortal residents began to put more and more stock in the stories of Beattie.

"She told me that one evening two of the girls were in the kitchen and thought they heard the door open," said the mother. "They mentioned hearing a swooshing sound. They looked up and saw a figure of a woman, all white, and she crossed the top of the steps and went right into the bathroom."

Those steps, and that bathroom, we will find out soon, have seemed to be the focal points in the story of Beattie over the years.

The girl's mother continued to tell the story. "We went up to visit her the first time, and that first time I actually felt the hair over my whole body stand up! I felt chills and a strange feeling."

Her experiences in the second-floor apartment were limited, when compared to those of her daughter and her roommates.

"My daughter was home alone one night," she related, "and she heard the door open and footsteps ascending the steps. She instinctively called out her roommates's name. 'Linda' she said, but got no response. She told me she definitely heard the footsteps, though."

What's more, the sound of the footsteps was soon accompanied by a more distressing phenomenon. As she mentally traced the upward sound of the footsteps on the stairs, she watched as a vague figure floated up the stairs, brushed by her with an unearthly swooshing sound, and disappeared into the bathroom at the top of the stairs.

"She said it was like seeing something on television," her mother later said. "It was there, and visible, but somehow it wasn't."

The girl described the apparition as a tall, thin woman clad in a white top and white slacks. The figure's hair was pulled up, and its face was that of a fairly young woman.

Just based on the flimsy features she could note under the circumstances, the student believed the spirit could have been that of a young woman who, in life, had been perhaps a nurse or beautician. She felt no ill will, no threat, and believed that the ghost had not departed its earthly plane very long ago.

Names are not particularly integral to this story, since several people, past and present, have added their own elements to the story of the ghost of Analomink Street.

As a student residence is wont to do, the house has seen a succession of tenants over the years. At the time this book was researched, its residents were two charming and lovely young women who were a bit put off by the knock on the door one Friday afternoon.

As we waited for a reply to our summon that day, we

wondered what would take place when we confronted those inside with the questions which had to be asked: "Do you know anything about the ghost that's supposed to be in your apartment?"

If it is hard to imagine moving in to a new, albeit temporary, home and discovering from prior residents that you will be living there with a ghost, it is equally difficult to imagine being informed of the ghostly cohabitant by two men who come to your door one afternoon.

Let us call the girls Kathy and Ashley. They may or may not be their real names, but again, names are not terribly germaine to the story.

Ashley came bounding down the stairs in response to the knock. She greeted the two ghost-hunting strangers with caution. "Hi, may I help you?"

After assuring her we were not insurance salesmen, cops, evangelists or bill collectors, we eased into our quest.

"This will be the strangest question you have been asked in a long time," we stated. How else can one preface a query about a ghost in the house?

"Go ahead," Ashley said, "try me."

"Ok, to get to the point, do you know anything about the ghost that's supposed to be in your apartment?"

Ashley's bright smile and peppy demeanor melted in a flash. She called upstairs for Kathy.

"What exactly do you mean," Ashley asked timidly.

"Your know, a ghost," we fumbled.

The verbal jousting continued briefly, and after more proper introductions and assurances that we might like to know more about we knew, Ashley and Kathy invited us in.

Ashley readily admitted that she had heard tales of the alleged "haunting of the house as she was moving in, but offered little else of substance at the start.

"Some of the guys who had lived in the house told us some pretty bizarre stories," she said. "At one time, they were at the kitchen table and they saw the figure of a woman coming out of the living room radiator."

After the expected chuckling died down, Ashley and Kathy agreed that the notion of a ghost seeping out of a

6

radiator is a bit far-fetched. But she continued the story as was told to her nonetheless.

"They said she went out of the radiator, and they said she was all white, with long, dark hair. They said they heard a swishing sound as she passed by. She passed by them, they told us, and rounded that corner into the bathroom."

The layout of the upstairs apartment may play a part in the ambling of the apparition.

The staircase angles up from the front door and leads almost directly into the bathroom. On the right is the living room and the radiator from which the former residents claim the spirit oozed.

A short hallway to the left leads to the kitchen, and a bedroom is located just off to the left at the top of the steps.

A relatively large, walled-in section separates the hall from the bedroom and seems to serve little architectural function. What could well have been a substantial closet space is nothing but a hollow, inaccessible void.

Ashley and Kathy never really noticed the empty space, but the ghost hunters readily discovered it and surmised it may have a role in the activities in the apartment.

Another suspect area in the apartment would be a small closet which is built into a living room wall which divides that room from the bathroom.

As it turns out, both spots indeed have been the sources of some mystery for Ashley and Kathy.

Ashley admitted, however, that only two unexplained incidents took place in the two months since they had moved in.

Kathy related one of them. It is interesting to note that when Kathy experienced what you are about to read, she had not yet been told of any stories regarding "Beattie" or any ghost in the apartment.

"I just got back from a weekend home," she said, "and we were siting around the place. I was leaning against the wall, talking on the phone. All of a sudden, I jumped. I know I heard something. It sounded like something inside the wall. We all jumped when I screamed. I know what I heard, and it scared me. It sounded like a high-pitched hum, and it wasn't like anything you'd hear from a house. It sounded like a human voice, coming from inside the wall."

Inside, we might add, the wall with the inexplicable empty space.

Ashley added another log to the frightening fire which has smoldered inside the house since the first reports of the ghost there began to circulate.

Occasionally, the door to the closet which is on the other side of the wall from the bathroom, will open with no human aid. Bulbs in a light fixture in the bathroom "live" for usually no longer than a week or so. And strange sounds have been heard from inside the vacant bathroom.

There is, too, a recurring rumor that a young woman did indeed die inside the bathroom, although nothing firm on that could be researched.

"This all sounds crazy," Kathy continued, "and maybe we're reading too much into some of this."

Maybe, Kathy, and maybe not.

Obviously, the old house has undergone many structural changes over the years. If there is any pattern to supernatural occurences, it is that in nearly every building your authors have investigated, some substantial renovations or alteration had been done to the property. Walls have been added or taken away. Steps had been built or removed. Open spaces had been closed, or closed spaces had been opened.

All of this may be may be meaningless, but there are very convincing theories from very credible researchers that such modifications in a home, new or old, may indeed touch off spirit activity.

The theory is at once ludicrous and logical.

As an example, one of the most profound ghost stories we have ever investigated takes place in an old house at the top of Hawk Mountain, Berks County, Pennsylvania. In that house, an apparition has been seen gliding about a foot and a half above the living room floor. Voices and strong psychic energy as determined by a medium have been detected in the middle of that living room floor.

This seemingly inocuous information becomes frighteningly important when it is documented that a young girl died in the house. She apparently fell down a flight of steps and broke her neck.

Shortly after the tragedy, the house was renovated. The steps, which were located at what is now the middle of the living room floor, were removed, and the entire floor of the room was lowered by eighteen inches.

Therefore, the psychic reading of the activity in the room, paired with the eyewitness account of the apparition (floating eighteen inches above the present floor level), and both of these added to the architectural alterations which were made, could prove meaningful.

Could not that strong "spiral of energy" which is emitted from the middle of the living room today emanate from the location of the fatal accident? Could not the fact that the spirit was gliding eighteen inches above the present floor level correspond to the fact that "it" is simply on a plane it knew before the changes were made?

It is believed by some serious researchers of the paranormal that the simplest of scientific principles could well harbor the answers to ghostly questions.

As one records music or voice in the recording process, one is simply recording energy onto nothing more than sophisticated rust.

That energy is virtually permanently recorded onto that rust, and serves no purpose until it is played back through other electronic means.

One explanation of the sights, sounds and sensations which accompany reports of "ghosts" is startling, but all to simple and plausible.

The human body contains electrical energy. It is what sparks our senses and makes us think, and react.

It is believed by some scientists that at the time of a traumatic experience, usually but not limited to death, this energy is literally burst out of the body.

In the case of a death, the body itself becomes a lifeless, energy-less corpse. The energy, according to the theory, is discharged into the atmosphere. Energy, as matter, cannot be destroyed.

It follows, then, that most of the energy disperses. But it is believed that some of it may indeed find a "recording" medium somewhere and bits and pieces of this human energy, memory, thought, etc., may actually imprint itself.

It could well be that the necessary medium is rust.

Thus, with those shards of information on that rust, wherever it may be in the location of the initial trauma, a receptive mind of a psychic or medium may become the "playback" mechanism and sense those bits and pieces of what was human energy.

Enhanced by the frailties, fears, innocence and imagination of the living receptor, that energy could be translated into sounds, motion or visions. The energy, expended, recorded and played back, becomes a ghost.

Right now, an East Stroudsburg University professor is reading this, and is ready to shoot off a letter to your authors. Don't bother, doc, the research is out there.

But all of this takes some of the fun out of a good, old ghost story. This book is not a scientific treatise or an history book. A book titled, "Pocono Energy Stories" would stand little chance of selling. The book is a compilation of ghost stories from the Pocono Mountains and Pocono people, and nothing more.

After a long day on the ski slopes, the bridle path, golf course or in the classroom, or after a hard day of work, the last thing you'd want to read is the "hows" and "whys" of ghosts. And, it's the last thing we would want to write about.

So relax, turn out every light but the one you're reading this by, and be prepared to experience the stories from the other side of life in the majestic Pocono Mountain region.

And if you should hear a scratching sound in the wall, its probably just a mouse. If you hear a wooshing sound, it's just the wind. If you feel an icy chill, check the furnace. If a glowing figure passes through the room, have your eyes examined.

None of this is real, is it?

Ghosts don't really exist, do they?

Your authors don't pretend, and do not wish to, have any answers. But if ghosts do not exist, and if all of this is so much bunk, try telling that to those who told their stories and made this book possible.

HAUNTED HILLS AND HOUSES

The most challenging type of ghost story the researcher faces is what we have come to call the "they say" story.

"They say" a ghost walks along a lonely stretch of Route 402 near Resica Falls. "They say" it is the sorrowful spirit of a young maiden, searching for her lover who was shot in a hunting accident.

Exactly where has her ghost been seen? When was her lover killed? What was the girl's name?

Alas, nobody knows for sure. But "they say" the story is true.

Who is "they?"

Although the facts can rarely be uncovered, and the "they" can almost never be identified, the "they say" story remains a powerful kind of ghost story which by its own unanswered questions become more mysterious and baffling.

After all, any legend in which every detail can be corroborated, every date confirmed and all t's crossed and i's dotted is no longer a legend.

A ghost story, by its very nature, should have vast

chasms of fact which must be leaped over or avoided in order to seperate itself from an historical account.

Throughout the Poconos, "they say" stories are in abundance. The roadside wraith of Resica Falls is an example. So is what "they" call the Spruce Woods Ghost.

In this case, at least one "they" can be identified. Claire Wellingford, operator of the Appenzell General Store, recalls the stories his grandfather, Clyde Paul, used to tell about the spooks of Spruce Woods, along Neola Road.

It was the ghost story of a campfire calibre. Folks thereabouts, whether they believed the yarns or not, still paused before wandering into the woods where "they say" the poor of a dead man still wanders after an untimely and, "they say," unspeakable death somewhere between the trees of Spruce Woods.

Was he hanged? Did he commit suicide? Was he murdered? Nobody really knows. But we do know that for Claire Wellingford, and many others around Appenzell, Spruce Woods was where a ghost was, and they didn't want to be.

Out on Preacher Hill Road, near Mountainhome and in a turn-of-the-century home, "they say" a ghost makes things disappear and then returns them after awhile. The same pesky phantom is responsible for quiet, eerie music which can be heard within the walls of the old house. Even the family dog there seems to respond to unseen commands and has been known to growl at invisible intruders.

The "they" in this story are the people who live in the house, and for reasons the authors respect declined to give their names.

Such is the case with another person in Greentown, in whose ninety year old home is a ghost which walks the floorboards of his second floor. Both he and his wife have heard the footsteps, and even their dog's ears have perked when the plaintive, steady footfalls begin.

Debbie Herman, who lived in a pleasant cottage along Rinker Road for a while, is more than eager to tell her story about her brush with the unknown.

13

It seems, or at least "they say" that a woman was making butter one day a long time ago and somehow her dress caught fire. She burned to death in the old house.

The woman loved roses, and loved to spend her relaxation times rocking in a chair in the parlor.

On several occasions while Debbie was living in the house, her own rocker would slowly begin to rock back and forth, as if someone was sitting in it. There was no breeze, no windows were opened, and nothing could logically explain the motion of the chair.

Another time, while Debbie was busy making Christmas cookies in the kitchen, she was distracted by a shadowy face staring at her through the kitchen window.

She recoiled, fearing there was a prowler about. She saw the face clearly, but did not recognize it. Besides, it was snowing outside at the time, and she wondered who would be outside on such a night.

She called for her husband, who came immediately to check on who was out there, looking in a window of their home.

He stepped outside cautiously and went to the window in which Debbie has seen the face.

Her husband came back into the house, shook the snow from his boots and told Debbie she must have been seeing things. There couldn't have been anyone standing at that window, looking inside. There were no foot prints whatsoever in the snow outside their house.

But Debbie knew what she had seen, and believed it to be but one thing . . . a ghost!

CHARLIE'S GHOST

If you were to imagine the most unlikely looking place for a haunting, you just might imagine a place such as the International Eatery, on Route 611 in Bartonsville.

Along a busy commercial highway, the tiny restaurant is set in a strip shopping center of relatively recent construction.

Clean, pleasant and welcoming as it is, the International certainly does not fit the format most folks have assigned to the scene of ghostly activities.

But don't tell that to Charlie Taylor, Ruth Zetelski or Dianne Oliviera.

Mr. Taylor is proprietor of the eatery, and provided some background information on the setting.

The highway frontage upon which the restaurant and shopping center is located was once part of a large parcel owned by a woman who lived in a substantial house in a wooded area behind the present location of the center, and a recreational complex.

In the late 1970s, the woman passed away, and her home burned to the ground in a blaze which was ruled suspicious in origin.

While it is set in bright, modern surroundings, the International Eatery is decorated to the taste of Charlie Taylor.

Impressive antique accessories complement the utilitarian dining room furnishings, and collectibles in turn grace the antique cabinets and curios.

In one corner of the dining room is a framed glossy

photograph of Frank Sinatra, signed, "To Charlie, from Frank Sinatra."

After expressing how impressed we were with his apparent closeness to "old blue eyes," Charlie chuckled and broke the bubble: "Got it at a flea market," he revealed.

His enthusiasm for antiques and collectables may or may not be germaine to what has been seen and felt inside his restaurant. There are some theories which claim that supernatural energy can remain embodied, so to speak, in furniture, and the furniture, not necessarily the room or building, can thus be the source of any "haunting."

Charlie Taylor does not rule out the possibility that a charming, old photograph collected at a flea market and setting on an antique desk may have something to do with the mysterious happenings in the eatery.

The picture is a portrait of three young women, each staring out of the sepiatone with fixed eyes and smiles captured forever on film.

What is known at the International Eatery is that more than a few people who work there or have passed through there have had experiences they simply could not explain.

The restaurant is airy and open. A low divider separates the two small dining rooms, and the small counter space is just steps away form the farthest corner of the eating area. Only the kitchen is in a completely separate room.

Charlie was first to provide testimony about what has happened in the place.

He was standing in the dining room by the cash register once when a vague, hazy figure in the shape of a woman passed from the kitchen door into walk-in cooler. "It walked, or glided, right into the cooler," he affirmed.

Astonished, confused, and probably a bit concerned, Charlie watched for another sign. There was nothing. It seemed to be an isolated incident, and it was a long period until the same vision made another appearance, and another, and another.

Charlie has seen the silent, shadowy figure on several occasions since that first encounter. There has never been a sound attached to it, and Charlie feels there is nothing sinister or evil about the apparition.

On one occasion, Charlie and three employees were mingling with a group gathered there for a party. One particular waitress, Betty Edienger, was chatting away with one of the patrons when she stopped in mid-sentence.

She stared toward the refrigerator near the counter, her eyes rivited to what she described later as the hazy outline of a woman.

Charlie Taylor recalled another episode which gives the ghost hunter pause for pondering.

"We have a friend from Connecticut," he said. "Her name is Dianne Oliviera and she comes down on Saturday nights and stays until Sunday night and works here on Sundays. One time, I took her car and went to the store.

"Dianne was sitting in a chair by the counter, and I was bringing the groceries in.

"I put them on the counter, and I had left the car trunk lid open. Nobody was out there.

"All of a sudden, Dianne said she saw someone go into the trunk of the car and take something out. Of course, I checked it out quickly. There was nobody there, and nothing was missing. But Dianne insisted there was someone there, as if they were trying to help take the groceries in."

Dianne later confirmed her experience, and swore that she saw a very vague, but very real figure out by her car that day.

Ruth Zetelski, who manages the restaurant for Charlie Taylor, has had her own encounter with the ghostly figure, and has even given it a name.

Taylor collects records from the 1930s and 1940s, and one of Ruth's favorites from his collection is "Veronica Plays Her Harmonica." For no other reason than that, she has come to call the ghost Veronica.

Ruth admitted that whenever the feeling that Veronica is present, the hair on her arms stand up. But she feels no fear. "It's like she's checking up on the place," she said. "She wants to make sure everything's OK."

Ruth describes the spirit as short in stature, silent, and wispy.

What she has seen on two occasions simply has simply stood either near the menu board or near the kitchen door. "It was cloudy around the edges, if you know what I mean," she recalled. "I saw a little bit of what I could describe as hair, but then it just zoomed, you know, it just disappeared. The top was the last part to vanish."

Nobody at the International Eatery is sure who their ghost may be, but most will venture the guess that it very well may be the deceased former owner of the land, bound forever to look after what once was hers.

MYSTERY IN MERWINSBURG

There's not much to Merwinsburg. The crossroads hamlet isn't far from busy Route 115, firmly entrenched in the rugged countryside in the west end of Monroe County. About twelve to fifteen people call it home.

And so does at least one ghost.

Such is the firm belief of Bill Shiffer, who owns and resides in what is arguably the most historic building in Merwinsburg.

The village is named for the Merwin family, which settled there in the middle of the eighteeth century. Their inn, then on the main highway from Easton to Wilkes-Barre, flourished for more than a century as a post office, stage coach stop, boarding house and summer resort.

The oldest part of the old Merwin house was built in 1756, and another section was added in about 1840.

Bill Shiffer knew the place well. He was born in the house just across the driveway from the Merwin place, and knew well the history of the old inn. He knew that some famous people, John James Audubon among them, supposedly stayed there, and knew that many happy and sad events had taken place there.

After the Merwin family had relinguished ownership of the inn, the Gould family took it over, and the last surviving Gould, Norma, was Bill's aunt. After inheriting the inn along with two others, Bill bought it and converted into his home in 1988.

By then, he already knew it was haunted.

Haunted by whom, he did not know. Haunted by what, however, was a well-known family story.

His mother, Claudia Shiffer, and aunt Norma Gould had often heard and seen their phantom cohabitant.

Eerie music could be heard wafting down a central corridor of the house. "The music sounded like it was coming from far away and long ago," he said.

What is particularly interesting about the ghostly music is that both Bill's mother and aunt had heard it, but not at the same time. They did not live in the house together, and reported hearing the music independent of one another. Both described the same phenomenon, however.

The mysterious music was not the only unexplainable event to take place in the old Merwinsburg Inn.

Bill's mother would swear she saw what she believed to be the spirit of Bill's uncle (her brother) in the house shortly after he passed away. "She told me she saw his ghost," Bill recalled. "She said it was a very vague outline, and she saw it in the hallway."

Ghostly images have also been seen in an upstairs room in which it is known several people have died.

The most memorable experience, and one Bill Shiffer has the least doubt about, was reported by his own daughter.

Sally Ann Shiffer said she saw the bizzare form in that upstairs room. She described it as all white, and wearing a tall, pointed, hat which she likened to a dunce cap.

While she said the ghost was not threatening, it still had her upset for several days after the first encounter.

THE GRAY LADY

It is a small, handsome home on the outskirts of
Mountain Home. Built in the 1920s, it is unremarkable and
hardly indicative of the common perception of a "haunted
house."

But it is within the walls of this simple suburban home
that the kindly ghost of the "gray lady" dwells.

"When we first moved here," the present occupant
said, "there was one room upstairs which always felt very
cold."

That occupant, whom we shall call Betty, is a talented,
artsy type who proceeded to transform the drab, old house
into a showcase for her skills.

"When we remodeled the house, I made another room
my daughter's bedroom. But she didn't like that because
she couldn't see our bedroom door down the hall from her
room. So, she wanted to move into that colder room. Well,
we put her there."

And then, said Betty, is when the presence of the mysterious woman made itself known.

"One night, my daughter came down the hallway and
tapped me and said, 'mommy, there's a lady in my room.' I
told her that was silly, that there was no lady in her room.
She said, 'Yes there is, mommy, she's a gray lady. She has
gray hair and she has a long nightgown on and she's in my
room and I don't like it.' "

Betty said she is not a non-believer in spirit activity.
She has remained open-minded on the subject, and has

21

always been prepared to meet head-on any encounter with a brush with the unknown. Still, this encounter was translated by her young daughter. The little girl's concern and confusion became hers, as well.

Betty continued to relate the story. "I could tell that she was afraid. So, I took her back into her room, turned on the lights and showed her there was nothing there. She went to sleep and everything was fine."

The solitude didn't last long, however.

"The next night," Betty continued, "she came down the hall and said, Mommy, that lady's back in my room again. But it's all right, mommy, because she likes me. She winked at me."

Betty tried to dismiss her daughter's observations as those of an impressionable, imaginative young girl. But inside her there were doubts. Doubts that her daughter would make up a tale such as this and stick with it as she had.

"She stayed in her room, and after she told me the woman, the ghost or whatever, winked at her, there was never a mention of the lady in gray for a long time.

Betty continued to remodel her home, and it appeared, perhaps, that her growing daughter may indeed have outgrown the stories of what was variously called the "gray lady" and "Mrs. Gray." for want of any better identification.

In candid conversation with neighbors and area elders, the usual stories surfaced: A woman had died in the house, in the yard, etc., etc. Nothing could be confirmed.

But the presence on the second floor of Betty's house made itself known soon enough.

"When my sister stayed with me one weekend, she saw somebody coming down the hall in a long nightgown."

There wasn't much more to it than that. The usual questions arose when Betty's sister reported the sighting. The women discussed the "gray lady" and resigned themselves to the fact that Betty's house is haunted.

"But she seems like a friendly person," Betty said. "I have never seen her, and I'd probably be scared to death if I would. Still, I believe my daughter and my sister, and if there is a ghost in here, and I believe there is, maybe it is of someone who once lived here and was concerned when we first moved in and made so many changes. Maybe we haven't heard or seen much of her in a while because she's pleased about what we've done."

A SPELL ON THE PIG

They call Claude Possinger "Boob." At the time of the interview, he was a lively septuagenarian and a Chestnut Hill Township supervisor. He was also one of those individuals within whom the legends of his locale and life reside.

As Boob opened his treasure chest of lore to the eager researchers, the search for ghosts in the hills and dales of the Poconos took a different tack. You see, Boob Possinger couldn't recall much about spooks and spirits, but he had a couple of tales from the area which focused on an equally fascinating, mysterious and frightening subject: Witches.

Witchcraft is a phenomenon which is, in some form or other, prevalent in virtually every society and civilization and every time period, from the very beginnings of recorded history to the present.

While it has been perceived by many people as "evil" and, "the work of the Devil," its influence within those societies has had a profound impact throughout history.

Pennsylvania has a very interesting connection with witchcraft, and in a more palatable but no less threatening form, what could be considered witchcraft has been a way of life in many sections of the state for many years.

To its extreme, witchcraft, or in the Pennsylvania German vernacular, "Hexerei," has been blamed on murders, family feuds and a litany of tragedies. Conversely, another practice which could be linked with witchcraft, "Pow-wow," has been an accepted form of quasi-medical treatment for centuries.

Pow-wowers still exist in some regions of Pennsylvania's "Dutch Country," and some people there visit these "pow-wow doctors" before they consult a medical doctor.

These faith healers and "witches" can be found mostly in York, Lancaster and Berks counties, and the sourcebook of their trade can be traced to an 84-page publication which came out of a small Reading print shop.

"The Long Lost Friend," or "Der Lang Verbogen Freund," was written by John George Hohman and made its bow on the literary scene in 1819.

More than a half-million copies of the book have been reprinted over the years in 150 editions. Re-prints are still available, but a first edition is considered very rare.

Hohman promised the reader, " . . . whosoever carries this book with him would be protected from drowning, burning and would avoid any unjust sentence passed upon him."

Hohman further offered dozens of cures and remedies which would relieve the reader of virtually every ailment known to man. For instance, for a toothache, simply take a thread and soak it with blood. Then, take vinegar and flour, mix them into a paste and spread some of the goo on a cloth. Wrap the cloth around the root of an apple tree and tie it lightly with the blood-soaked thread. Then, cover the root with soil. The toothache will subside.

Cures, curses, potions and preventions have long been offered by those who claim to be in command of a divine providence. People have lived and died by those claims, and their folklore as a people has been enriched by them as well.

Take, for example, Boob Possinger's story of the bewitched pig.

At least that's how the tale has been passed down through the generations.

In fact, it was Boob's "granny" who was blamed for the bewitching of the animal. It seems there was a man named Miller who lived on a farm along Possinger Road, on the border of Jackson and Pocono townships, near what is now a sprawling truck terminal along Route 715.

Miller tried his hand at butchering his pigs on the property, but he told neighbors he would "stick the pig, and it wouldn't die." He claimed somebody put a spell on his pigs, and that somebody, for some reason, was Boob Possinger's grandmother.

They say Mr. Miller even bore holes in tree trunks and took thick locks of hair from his children's heads and stuffed them into the holes. He then sealed the hole with a wooden peg, in an effort to frustrate the witch.

A variation of this bizarre procedure was revealed previously in Monroe County folklore, and a relic of it is on display at the county historical society museum in Stroudsburg.

In her Halloween, 1988, article, "Tales from the Dark Side," writer Patricia Warren detailed the stories of several incidents of witchcraft, including that which relates to the "hair in the hole."

The tree trunk at the historical society has precious few strands of human hair left stuffed within it, but Warren credits the late Margaret Van Why of East Stroudsburg with an explanation of how it all came about.

Warren wrote that Van Why said the hair, found deep within a large, mature tree in the 1920s by members of the Saw Creek Club who were splitting firewood, belonged to her sister, Libby Jane (Counterman) Miller, "and placed in the tree to ward off the spell of a witch."

Libby was the daughter of a former owner of the property, and, as Warren continued, "One day, when she was working at the neighboring Millers' home, she was seized with a spell, which brought on paralysis and struck her dumb.

"Van Why directed a lock of Libby's chestnut hair be cut and hidden in the oak tree.

"On the following day, Van Why said she, her brother, and two cousins saw a large, strange animal near the tree. They summoned some men, but by the time they arrived, there was no sign of the animal or its tracks."

The "cure" apparently worked, as the young woman's

malady cleared, and there was never again a hint of any spells or bewitchings.

Whether the "Miller" mentioned in the Warren story is the Miller of Possinger Road has been lost in the fog of folklore. But the latter Miller's problem with witches wasn't resolved with the old "hair in the hole" trick.

One time, Mr. Miller fell out of an apple tree, and broke his arm. He blamed that incident on a chap who lived below Reeders. He had put a spell on him, and that's why he took the plunge from the tree limb.

Even the chickens in the barn fell victim to Miller's fears and superstitions. It's said that one night, he was walking past the barn when he heard a strange moaning sound coming from within. Thinking it was the plaintive sighs of the witch, he grabbed his shotgun, aimed into the barn, and blew a flock of cooing chickens to that big coop in the sky.

Things got so bad for the fellow that he eventually moved from the farm because of the hexes, spells, curses and witches.

Claude Possinger's own childhood memories harken back to stories of witches at his own aunt's farm, also on Possinger Road.

People would come from as far as Stroudsburg to try to catch a glimpse of the goblins or witches who were said to inhabit the barn there. They say strange forms would shoot over the cow manger, and strange, unearthly sounds could be heard coming from inside the barn at night. They were not, all knew, the sounds of a barnyard.

It was in the 1920s, and going to the old farm to seek spooks was good, clean fun for many folks in the area. Some claim they saw eerie lights inside the barn at night, and others said they could rid the place of its witches by shooting silver bullets into the barn. Nobody really ever did that, as best as Boob Possinger can recall.

Even Gertrude Possinger, Claude's wife, recalls the stories about the barn from their childhood. She especially remembers tales of fireballs soaring out of the barn, and rumors that a man was murdered inside it. That murder, some said, was what started the "haunting" or "bewitching" of the barn.

The people who own that property today have heard the stories from those days of old, and take them somewhat seriously. However, only the stone foundation from the old barn survived a fire several years ago, and nothing since that blaze has happened to keep the fires of this particular folk tale fanned.

RESORT WRAITHS

When researching the legends of the Pocono Mountains, it is interesting to discover how the storied history of the region often blends with the present culture and commerce of the area.

Since the first resort hotels were built under the watchful and temperant eyes of the Quakers, the direction of the development in the mountains has shifted from logging, tanning and other industries which helped scalp the hills of much of their natural bounty to, like it or not, a strong service economy. The resorts of the Poconos are the seasonal bedrooms and playrooms of honeymooners, families and outdoor sports enthusiasts from all over the northeast and beyond.

In the decades since the opening of that first resort, much of the natural and, for our purposes, supernatural allure of the region has been gobbled up by the investment companies which have laid claim to their sprawling swaths of prime Pocono countryside.

While the thirst for profits has too often been quenched with careless development, there are shining examples of how thoughtful developers managed to preserve and protect the heritage of the Poconos.

The 2,200-acre luxury Shawnee Inn, adjacent to the village of the same name, has spread its golf course, ski slopes and villas along the shore of the Delaware River and beyond. Built in 1912, the Shawnee Inn was once the Buckwood Inn, and was purchased in 1943 by noted musician (and blender inventor) Fred Waring.

For all its size, Shawnee has taken some measures to preserve Indian diggings along the river and Brodheads Creek, and has retained what is considered the first permanent white settlement in Monroe county as an office building.

The resort has published a brief history of its property, in which it states: "The building now known as the Fort Depuy Building was built in 1726 as the main dwelling within Fort Depuy, housing the Jacob Depuy family."

Now used as the central office for a cluster of elegant, riverside timeshare homes, the magnificent brick building stands at the end of a long lane which extends from River Road. The Delaware flows majestically to its rear, and the hills of New Jersey are its backdrop.

By day, the office is a busy place, but after the sun sets, even the hardiest of mortals would rather be somewhere else than within its walls.

Old Fort Depuy is haunted.

At least two security guards, one a night watchman on the Depuy Village grounds, have had brushes with strange sights and sounds inside the building.

The place is apparently inhabited by the restless ghost of a woman. One of the guards says he saw her. He didn't want his name mentioned, but he was quite open with his story. "This place is weird, spooky, at night," he said. "I've been in here, alone, with all the doors closed and everything, and I have heard footsteps.

"I knew it wasn't some other kind of noise old houses might make," he continued. "It was most definitely the sound of feet walking across a floor. I tell you, I'd rather be anywhere else but here sometimes, but it's my job, so what can I say?"

The security guard added that others have reported feeling an icy chill pass by them with a "whooshing" sound. Inside doors, known to be securely locked, have opened on their own, and one man who works at the office says he has seen the ghostly form of a woman walking across a second floor corridor and through walls there.

Another portion of the Shawnee Inn property has a supernatural connection, but those expecting to see a mysterious Gothic house high on a windy hill will be disappointed.

Where the old "haunted house" once stood is now the sign which heralds the Shawnee Mountain Ski Area.

Susie Wyckoff, who operates the well-stocked Shawnee General Store in the village, eagerly shared her knowledge and her pride for the area which has been her family's home for generations.

One of the stories she recalled was that of the old neighborhood "haunted house," which was out on Hollow Road, at the present entrance to the ski area parking lot.

It was the kind of place kids rode their bikes past very quickly. It was the kind of place nobody ever lived in very long, because, it was generally conceded, the house was infested with ghoulies and ghosties and things that went bump in the night.

Usually vacant, boarded-up, and uninviting, the narrow, three-story frame house earned its dubious reputation with equally dubious evidence.

Whatever fears, suspicions and superstitions doomed the place to its role in the community were flimsy, but effective. Folks young and old around Shawnee remember the old "haunted house on Hollow Road."

Elnora Houser says the stories have been circulating around those parts for more than sixty years. It is said somebody committed suicide by hanging themself out on the back porch of the house a long time ago, and some say the place was possessed by demons.

Elnora recalled one incident which loosely relates to the old house. She said a friend took a roll of pictures which included two shots of the old haunted house.

When the pictures were processed, every photo except the two of the house came out beautifully. The two shots of the house, taken under normal circumstances and light conditions, were totally blank.

Another of the grand dames of Pocono resorts is, or was, The Inn at Buck Hill Falls. Built in 1898, the inn was closed at the time of this writing.

A very thorough security force patrols the inn and its grounds, and Tom Buckmann, one of the officers on the site, told of the reported ethereal activities inside the building.

"There was always talk of a ghost being up in one of the rooms on the second or third floor," he said. "They'd be cleaning there and the door would close behind them and the curtains would blow, even when the windows were all closed. Some of the maids got so they wouldn't even go in that room anymore," he concluded.

On Evergreen Road, near Canadensis is the lovely Pines Hotel, built in 1908.

Billy Helbig, a part owner of the Pines, is the fourth generation of the family which built the hotel, and with mother Hilde at his side, Billy told of the ghost or ghosts which roam the rooms and grounds of his hotel.

"One of the chambermaids," he said, "was cleaning a bath tub in one of the cottages. She was of Indian descent, and was very much in tune with the lore of her ancestors.

"As she was scrubbing the tub," he continued, "she looked around and saw what she described to us as a tall, handsome ghost."

Billy described the spirit as being well dressed, about six feet, two inches tall, with black hair.

He said, "The maid said to him 'well, are you just going to stand here, or are you going to get over here and help me?' He just stood there, unresponsive, and she advised him to leave, and he did."

Billy said the maid told him the hotel and its grounds, which incidentally wrap around an old graveyard, are "loaded with ghosts." Although she never really elaborated on her claim, she did admit that even she was afraid to be by herself in some of the rooms there.

As any self-respecting, innovative and, well, courageous keeper of an inn with ghosts might well do, Billy has capitalized somewhat on the alleged otherwordly atmosphere at the Pines. Part of the entertainment program for children throughout the summer season is an optional "fright night," in which ghost stories are told and spooky stunts are carried out.

Legends and one peculiar story which may become legend, abound within the confines of the largest landowner in Monroe county, Skytop.

The Skytop Lodge was built in 1928 by New York City securities dealer John Stubbs, who found the nearby Quaker-run Buck Hill Falls hotel to be a bit stodgy.

After assembling the necessary financial backing, Stubbs and his investors proceeded to buy some 5,500 acres and carve out a challenging golf course and all the other requisite recreational facilities of a luxury resort.

But with all the building, much of the natural beauty of the spread was preserved, and in some cases, enhanced.

William W. Malleson is president and general manager of Skytop Lodge, and he knows well the stories that go with some of the natural wonders at Skytop.

"Where the trout stream comes down, there's Indian Ladder Falls," he said. Incidentally, renowned author Wallace Nutting, once called Indian Ladder, "the most beautiful falls in Pennsylvania."

But Mr. Malleson says there is a kind of tragic beauty even in how the falls got their name.

"The legend has it here," he continued, "that back in the 1700s, there were Indian raids here. And, of course, there's no question about that. Supposedly, some of the Indians and settlers clashed right here, and the settlers chased the Indians up the valley, to where our trout stream is located. When they reached the falls, they literally climbed up the rocks of the falls and got away. That's why they're called the Indian Ladder Falls."

The Tout Stream Trail, extends nearly a mile from a parking area along Route 390, and the falls are 1.8 miles from the Skytop Lodge, accessible only on foot.

Malleson said there is another more contemporary tale about Skytop. It is, at best, a borderline ghost story, but nonetheless is a saga on how a couple came back from the dead, so to speak, to spook some of the folks at Skytop.

It seems that a couple came to Skytop many years ago on their honeymoon, and were so pleased with the service and amenities there that they returned year after year thereafter. It is a true story, and in deference to the family's privacy, we will not reveal the names of the couple. Let us call them Marv and Marsha. They became regulars at Skytop, and known well to all from top management to the household staff. A few years ago, however, Marv died. Marsha died a couple of years after Marv, and, needless to say, neither would ever be seen again at Sky-top.

Sort of.

Mr. Malleson took up the story from that point.

"In 1989," he recounted, "two of our department heads were out playing golf one day on our course and they came to the fifteenth tee. They looked over on the side, and there was this pile of stuff.

"They looked at it, and looked at it, and they walked over, took their golf clubs and prodded it. It looked like ashes, but they really didn't know what it was. They did notice two metal tags, though. They picked up the tags and they had numbers and a business name on them.

"They gathered the debris together, brought it back to the office, called me, and we discovered the business was a crematorium. Marv and Marsha had come back one more time!"

Malleson explained how Marv and Marsha had managed to return in ashen form to Skytop. "As it turned out," he said, "the executrix of the estate was instructed by Marv and Marsha that when both of them had passed away, their ashes were to be scattered over the grounds of Skytop Lodge, where their marriage began.

"When the executrix came to carry out that last wish, she panicked and left poor Marv and Marsha in one lump on the fifteenth tee.

"Later on, we obliged Marv and Marsha. We scattered their ashes over the fifteenth fairway, and we always say the fifteenth has never been greener!"

A GOOD GHOST

"Freaky . . . really freaky." Thus is the summation of one young woman who has experienced the sounds and sights of the spectral inhabitant of the Meisse home on Fenner Avenue in Sciota.

The events which have played out in the house are simple enough, but when compounded as they have, amount to a chain of events which is, well, "freaky . . . really freaky."

Skeptics, and those who either doubt, deny or have never experienced the energy and power of the supernatural, may read the following inventory of the unexplained in the Meisse home and wonder what all the fuss has been about.

But one should only be reminded to put it all in proper perspective. Imagine, if you will, that all you are about to read which happened in the Meisse house happened to you, in your house.

Imagine lying in bed one night, knowing you are alone in the house, and hearing footsteps cross back and forth in the hallway. You rise cautiously to investigate and see nothing. Still, the footsteps pace by you.

Imagine watching an apparent fully formed person walking gliding by your bed and vanishing into thin air as you watched.

Imagine you are listening as the bath tub spigot turned itself on and started to fill the tub.

Imagine watching a rocking chair slowly begin to rock

with no human aid or breeze.

These are the sorts of things which have happened to the Meisses. But Ralph Meisse Sr. is philosophical. "It's a good ghost," he says. "It takes care of us."

Meisse offers no apologies for his admitted belief in ghosts. "I have always believed in them" he says.

Indeed he should, if the events in his 125-year old house are any indication.

Most of the activity emanates from a second floor room and hallway. Wife Sandra, son Ralph Jr., daughters Heather and Danielle and even Buddy the dog have had their share of brushes with things that went bump, thump and swish in the night.

Perhaps most disquieting of all that has happened there took place just prior to the authors' visit to the Meisse home.

"We heard a baby cry," said Ralph Sr., "Just the other night, my wife and I were in the back room. We were both sitting there and we heard a baby call out her name."

One of Danielle Meisse's friends, Chris Lockie, had a similar experience during a "sleepover" in the house. She said she has gone to bed there and has heard what she thought was Danielle talking. The closer she listened, the more it sounded like someone crying. She was so curious that she got up, walked down the hall to see who it might be, and found nobody. Still, the crying continued and seemed to build in loudness and intensity. Chris has since declined invitations to stay the night.

By this time, though, the Meisse family has become almost oblivious to the sounds of their home. But that's not so with some who come to visit.

Cindy Bird, Sandra's aunt, has also heard and seen things she'd rather not while in the house. Once, when babysitting, she watched in stunned amazement as the living room light suddenly turned itself on. The upstairs bathroom light once did the same.

Cindy has also taken passes on offers to spend a night or two at her relatives' otherwise friendly and welcoming home.

It is interesting to note the lineage of the house. Sandra's father grew up in that house, and died in that house.

Actually, the house goes back another generation, and during that time, more than one resident has passed away in rooms there.

One, Sandra's aunt, is believed to have died in the room which is now Ralph Junior's bedroom.

It has been from and in that room that much of the unexplained sounds have originated, and the senior Mr. Meisse does not dismiss the possibility that the ghost he is certain walks the floors of his home may be that of the deceased relative.

And that is why Meisse believes the ghost is kindly, and, in fact, keeping watch over the family.

Phantom footsteps are a common occurrence in young "Ralphie's" room. As a youngster, Ralphie remembers being tucked into bed by unseen hands and watching as a vague figure crossed in front of his bed.

His father has also, almost, seen the elusive wraith.

"Oh, yeah," he says, "you'd see it, but you didn't, if you know what I mean. You would see something out of the corner of your eye, and you knew there was something there, but, well, you know."

Probably the most telling of all incidents which took place there took place as the family was putting up the Christmas tree one year. The children were toddlers at the time, and Ralph and Sandra always feared that the young ones would accidentally poke their eyes into the long needles of the blue spruce trees they always had.

That fateful Christmas, the parents' fears were within a hair's breadth of coming true as one of the little girls lost her balance while trimming the tree and started to fall into the tree.

In a flash, however, and as Ralph was snapping a picture, the girl righted herself as if an invisible arm had prevented her fall.

To the family's astonishment, when the photograph was developed, the faint outline of a human figure could be seen between the tree and the girl. Its feet, knees and hips were fairly evident, and there seemed to be an arm extended around the girl's body.

That was the Meisse house ghost, Ralph truly believes.

And while the family thinks of its resident spirit as benevolent, there are many friends who take a less optimistic attitude.

"There are so many people who have experienced something in this house," says Ralph Meisse Sr. "Whatever it is in here definitely seems to be watching over us."

But as Cindy Bird put it, good ghost or not, what has happened to her can be described in one phrase:

"Freaky . . . really freaky."

THE HENRYVILLE HAUNTING

The old Henryville Inn, once the gathering place of presidents and dignitaries, is, at the time of this writing, a lifeless hulk at the intersection of Routes 715 and 191.

This corpse of a resort, where only vague vestiges of its past glories can be discerned, has all the trappings of what the average person would consider a "haunted house."

Its grounds have been sullied with the discards of man and the overgrowth of nature. A once-splendid swimming pool is a crumbling crater. Sheds and outbuildings are ramshackled. Hundreds of windows, from which guests once gazed, are now hollow. Shreds of curtains flap in the breeze in some, and spiders spin intricate webs in others.

Little imagination is needed to conjure up the ghosts which may walk its long, empty corridors.

A bona fide historical landmark, the Henryville Inn once hosted the likes of Theodore Roosevelt and Harry Truman, and was one of the fine resorts of the Pocono past.

In more recent times, however, the old inn has become better known for its invisible guests who have been doomed to spend an eternity within its walls.

There are several tales which purport to provide a baseline for the haunting of Henryville.

A longtime neighbor just down the road from the inn tells the story of a former resident of the place who ended her life by dousing a bale of hay with gasoline, lighting it, and leaping into the inferno.

It is said the ghost of this woman has been seen in the

Henryville Inn, and has been known to shake boarders and visitors out of bed with her ghostly Reveille.

Another story circulated in the area is that of a destitute maid of the hotel who stood on a step leading to the basement, affixed a noose around her neck and jumped down. Her neck snapped, and her spirit was committed to the inn forever.

Whatever the source of the ghostly goings-on at Henryville, the reports of those who have come into contact with the spirits are legion.

One young woman who intended to take a job as the live-in caretaker at the inn before it slid into further disrepair, was frightened away by a combination of technical and logistical matters and the strong rumors that the sprawling old resort was haunted.

She said the human reasons were the main reasons for not taking the job, but admitted the supernatural stories did play a role in the rejection.

She heard the tales of workers there who were securing the property after it had closed, and were awakened as their beds began to shake violently.

Furthermore, while claiming no profound psychic powers, she said she sensed the presence of at least three ghosts in the place when she surveyed the buildings and land as she contemplated the caretaker's position.

Carl Perry, who keeps an eye on the old inn for those who owned it at the time of this writing, has certainly heard the many stories of the Henryville haunting, and has had his own uneasy feelings and experiences while making his rounds as guardian.

Perry says he was told a woman committed suicide on the fourth floor of the main inn, and has heard the other stories related to the suicides elsewhere in the structure.

He recalls the typical teen-years tales of things that went bump in the night there, but can cite more credible accounts as well.

There was once a caretaker there who claimed the unexplained, eerie sounds he would hear in the building were unbearable at time. At first, the noises were frightening.

Later, he would counter them by turning his stereo louder. Then, he became oblivious to them and managed to ignore them. He said they were not the sounds of an old building, nature or anything he could recognize readily. They were sounds from the spirit world.

Carl Perry says he always feels there is something or somebody in the building when he patrols it. He has heard the tinkling of glass and other sounds, and has occasionally made a hasty departure from the old inn.

He recalls, too, a woman who came there, looking into the possibility of buying the property. She examined the place closely, and might have purchased it. That is, until she detected the presence of the ghosts of a young girl and an older woman there.

What will happen to the grand old Henryville Inn is anyone's guess. It is well protected from intruders by security, and by presences which are perhaps more powerful and more frightening than any security guard ever could be.

Ghosts.

GHOSTS, MYTHS AND UFOs

In this chapter, we shall cover a broad spectrum of unexplained and perhaps unexplainable incidents which have taken place in the Pocono Mountain region over the years.

In the process of researching the stories for this book, several well-intentioned folks confused the study of Unidentified Flying Objects sightings with the study of the paranormal.

More often than not, those people asked if we knew about the strange UFO incident which catapulted the region into the national spotlight for a brief period.

While it is not germane to ghosts, the episode on March 1, 1973, will never be forgotten by those who experienced it.

The call came in to the Pennsylvania State Police dispatcher at Stroudsburg at about 9:30 that night. A Saylors Lake woman reported seeing about 40 unidentifiable objects hovering over the lake at an altitude of between 500 to 2,000 feet.

The circular objects glowed either red or white, and made no sound.

The woman who reported them to the state police told them later that several neighbors had been observing the lights for about two hours before the call was made.

A state trooper who went to the scene to investigate confirmed there were several objects flying over the lake, and could not identify them.

Contact was made with air traffic controllers in New York and the Willow Grove Naval Air Station, and these parties confirmed there was nothing on their radar screens in the Saylors Lake vicinity at that time.

Two days later, a Saylorsburg man called the state police once again, reporting more UFOs over Saylors Lake.

This time, three state troopers responded, and theorized the objects were high-flying airplanes.

There were several more reports of UFOs made in Monroe, Northampton and Lehigh counties in the next several weeks, and their validity was never challenged.

Strangely enough, as this book was being researched, another significant UFO sighting was reported to Chip Decker, an investigator affiliated with the Pennsylvania Association for the Study of the Unexplained.

"Again, water was involved," he said, noting that water is often associated with such sightings.

But this time, the water was in the form of two small lakes along Route 715 near Reeders, Jackson Township.

It was about 8 o'clock the night of February 4, 1991, when two women and their two daughters reported three separate sightings of what were described as large, silent, hovering crafts.

"They had mass," said Decker, "and they said they were rectangular in shape, with rows and rows of white lights with intermittent red lights in between."

Decker and fellow UFO prober Stan Gordon say these shapes and kinds of unidentified flying objects are what are called "box car UFOs," and what was seen by the four females that night is part of a worldwide trend of similar sightings.

Decker was called as the objects were being observed by the women that night, and he bolted out of his home, camcorder in hand, to the scene.

"Of course, I got there too late," he lamented. Local police responded to the report, as well, but they too saw nothing. Decker learned later that police in Mt. Bethel, Northampton County, received a similar call around the same time that night.

Decker's investigation followed all normal procedures. The witnesses were asked to provide separate hand drawings of what they had seen, they were thoroughly questioned and all area aviation authorities were asked about any unusual radar or operational occurrences.

The women were very excited about what they had seen, and seemed to be quite sincere and honest.

Air traffic controllers at airports in Allentown and Scranton reported nothing was awry in their regions that night, and contact was made to FAA officials and the Tobyhanna Army Depot. No unusual aircraft or radar contacts were reported in the area.

In addition to the unexplained and the unidentified, the unexpected has also played a role in life in the Poconos.

At a Marshalls Creek-area peat mining job site in the summer of 1968, workers were astounded when the massive bones of a mastodon were unearthed some 12,000 years after the animal's death.

The full skeleton of the rare American Mastodon was recreated by experts, and is on display at the William Penn Museum in Harrisburg.

The find by some boys and girls at Buttermilk Falls many years ago was a bit more unsettling.

Bill Vail, who is part of the crew that keeps the grounds of Bushkill Falls the pleasant place it is, remembers the time several youngsters were playing at the falls when one of them happened to reach his arm deep through the tumbling waters.

Against the rocks, he felt a peculiar stone, which he pulled out from behind the falls.

It was not a stone.

It was a skull.

His eyes the size of egg whites, the lad's shaking hand calmly placed the bony head back behind the waters, and not-so-calmly scurried away in utter fear.

THE INDIAN MUSEUM GHOST

Long before tourists came to gawk at Bushkill Falls, Indians bathed and frolicked in its rushing waters.

Long before skiers took to the slopes of Pocono peaks, Indians held sacred ceremonies on their lofty heights.

Tourists and time-sharers have forever changed the Poconos, and much of the lore of the Lenni Lenape has been lost in the shuffle of development.

One enterprise in the very heart of the Poconos' present has preserved some of the Poconos' past in the same building that serves the Poconos' future.

Along Route 209, just north of Marshall's Creek and near the crossroads village of Bushkill, is the Pocono Indian Museum. Or is it the Starting Gate Ski Shop?

Marge and Mal Law are no dummies. They have split the two major seasons of the Poconos into two ventures. A bright sign, pastel and fluorescent window displays and a breezy, sporty look mark the ski equipment and apparel business. A more subdued and dignified facade signifies the entrance to the Indian museum.

When the autumn leaves fall and the "think snow" crowd begins to assemble in the mountains, the action shifts to the ski shop. As the winter white melts into a spring green, the fair weather tourists begin their quest for diversions and the Indian Museum becomes the Laws' big draw. Both sides of the stately old building with the tall, white pillars are open year-round.

The building itself is a museum of sorts. Built in 1840

as the homestead of John Van Campen Coolbaugh, the much-expanded old home has a checkered past.

It served as a way station in the "underground railroad" of freed slaves, served stage coaches and teamsters in its position as a stop along the old Milford Road, and became notorious in the area as a brothel and barroom early in this century. During its heyday in that role, the "Joan of Arc" speakeasy, as it was known during Prohibition, played host to the likes of gangsters Dutch Shultz and Legs Diamond, who spent time there during visits to nearby boxing and gambling venues.

But the history of the building pales when compared to the history in the building. It took about a century and a half to compile the building's past, while the collection inside dates back thousands of years.

Display cases contain centuries-old pottery and other items from the Delaware Indians of the immediate area, depictions of the lifestyles of the Native Americans, and hundreds of artifacts collected in a region generally no farther than a twenty-mile radius of Bushkill.

But the ski shop and museum aside, what is even more intriguing about the old building is the fact that it is home for a ghost.

What the public sees as it streams through the cozy museum galleries or into the ski shop are only small portions of the building. Upstairs and downstairs are dark, foreboding chambers where all sorts of human drama have played out over the decades. One may only speculate as to what may have taken place there.

"I've heard it when I open up in the morning," one clerk said when asked about the ghost of the Indian Museum. "It's a creepy place when you're alone," she continued.

Mal Law agrees, while quickly noting that despite its eeriness, the old place has character.

Of that there can be no doubt. And, while several people say they have sensed, heard and even seen the ghost there on occasion, not one has felt threatened.

"When we opened as a museum," Mal said, "I would be working in the place at night alone. I would hear footsteps, and I would feel as if there was someone there with me. I knew I was alone, but I would still call out for my wife, and of course, nobody would answer."

Marge Law said she often senses a presence of an unseen being in the place, and her son, M. J., not only has those same feelings, but claims to have seen the faint image of whoever may be haunting the Indian Museum.

A cluttered room above the ski shop has served as a storage area and workshop. A trap door leads from the sales floor to the workshop room, through which merchandise can be handed down.

One night, M. J. Law was working alone in the workshop when he head the disembodied footsteps. He cocked his ear to listen closer, and glanced toward the door to the hallway. It was there he saw a figure pass by and disappear.

M. J. says he felt a surge of emotion which ranged from surprise to confusion. Fear was not among the emotions.

"Yeah," says Mal Law, "it can be a scary place at night, or when you're alone here. But we are not really frightened. We've even named our ghost 'Eli.' We still hear the footsteps, have those unexplainable feelings, and all that. But we're convinced that whoever or whatever is here is a good spirit. Maybe it's just here to watch over our place, to sort of protect it. At least that's what I'd like to think."

A SIGN FROM THE CORPSE

An enduring mystery in the Sand Hill area of Hamilton Township, Monroe county, is the brutal, unexplained and unsolved Halloween, 1880, murder of Etna Bittenbender.

Young Etna, eldest daughter in Sam Bittenbender's family, went to visit a neighbor just before dark. She promised to return home a bit later in the evening, and was in bright spirits when she left.

Etna cut through a wooded area near the road between Sand Hill and Neola, and met her destiny there at the cruel hands of an unknown assailant.

Unaware that his daughter had been cut down by a murderer, Sam Bittenbender tended to farm chores while Etna was ostensibly visiting the neighbors. As he carted a load of firewood along the roadway, he was oblivious to the fact that he passed by his girl's battered body.

The body was eventually discovered by Etna's brothers and sisters, who were returning home from the Reese School.

It is remembered by some who heard the story passed

49

down through their families that it may have been the ghost of Etna Bittenbender which led them to her corpse.

They say the body was hidden in thick underbrush near a stone fence along the road. The girl's head had been caved in by a solid wooden club, which was later found nearby.

But as the Bittenbender children's team of horses carried them along their way, they reared up at the precise location of the grisly remains. It is said the animals sensed the presence of the girl's beckoning spirit, which caused them to pause in fear and lead the brothers and sisters to the grim discovery.

A suspect was rounded up by police a few weeks later, but not enough evidence was secured to convict him.

The Etna Bittenbender murder, and the possibility of her ghost still haunting the road from Sand Hill to Neola, remains a tasty morsel of mystery in southern Monroe County.

THE CIDER PRESS GHOST

On the Neola Road near Appenzell, is a time-worn frame building which was once a cider mill.

Driving by the place, you'd hardly notice it. A stucco house stands behind the old press, and it, too is unremarkable within its rugged, rural setting.

But to those who live near the cider press and in the house adjacent to it, much in the way of remarkable has taken place there.

Rosa Rutherford, who resides nearby, said it was a bitter cold December night in the mid 1960s when she happened to check on her reclusive neighbor, James.

She ventured across the way, and while it was evident that the man's dog was secure in the warmth of the home, James was nowhere to be found.

She made one final check around the side of the house, and it was there where she made a grim discovery and saw a sight she will never forget.

"He was laying there by the house," Rosa said, "frozen stiff as a board. Rats had chewed his face, nose and mouth," and he was dead for a while."

Rosa recalled that the last time he was seen alive was three days before she discovered his frozen corpse. The man's faithful dog was still inside the old house as its master's body lay frozen in the snow.

Since then, the house at which the man died has been the site of mysterious events.

Robert Buzzard, who was renting the place at the time of this writing, says both he and his wife, Katrina, have had brushes with the unknown there.

Their house stands behind the now-abandoned cider mill, and in it is where Katrina has long sensed the presence of a ghost.

"At night, she'd actually see the spirit itself," says Robert Buzzard. "It is a lady."

The ghostly form would wander freely and aimlessly through the bedroom door and into the living room. It repeats this lonely pacing time and time again.

Mr. Buzzard claims his dog, a German Shepherd-collie mix named Benji, has also perked up, cocked its head, and obviously sensed the unearthly interloper.

"They say an animal can sense these things," Mr. Buzzard says, correctly.

Conversely, another spirit the Buzzards have detected in their home is that of a dog, which has been seen on occasion resting on the living room floor.

SUICIDE RIDGE

This story is not pleasant. The chapter title should be a dead giveaway (no pun intended) to that fact.

Originally, what is now Bonser Road just northwest of Saylorsburg in Ross Township, Monroe county, was the Sullivan Trail. Later, it was the Wilkes-Barre to Easton Turnpike.

Today, it is itself a ghost of its glory days as a main north-south route, and has become known locally by the rather ominous epithet as Suicide Ridge or, as some prefer, Hanging Ridge.

Either way, it is a bleak reference point for the stretch of roadway.

Oscar and Catherine Bonser live on the road whose name they share, and Oscar, 90 years old at the time of the interview for this book, remembers well how the ridge came to earn its gloomy nicknames.

The Depression of the 1930s hit the rural area there very hard. Farmers and factory workers struggled to make enough money to put food on their tables, and most managed to ride out the tough economic times.

Others were overburdened with financial woes and emotional problems, and chose to put an end to it all with a noose.

According to Oscar Bonser, the most notable suicides on the ridge included a man who hanged himself from a sturdy tree, and was followed later by his son. They were the Werkheisers, who farmed land on the ridge. "I don't know, they must have been crazy," said Oscar Bonser.

The Werkheiser suicides are but two of a string of tragedies which have given Suicide Ridge or Hanging Ridge its notoriety.

Emma Finkbeiner, who has lived in the area for many years, said black humorists years ago repeated, "If you want to hang yourself, go to Saylorsburg."

Emma recalled the old phrase with a sardonic chuckle, and talked of those who, many years ago, would spread tales that they would see folks walk by with a piece of rope in their hand on the way to Suicide Ridge. "But you know how stories like that go," she added. "That's all just a legend."

What is more than legend are the numerous suicides which have been carried out on or near the ridge. Bill Sobers, who with his father operates Sobers Meat Market on Old Route 115, recalled the Werkheiser suicides, another hanging in the Saylorsburg playground, and the carbon monoxide suicide of a man in a garage nearby.

Emma Finkbeiner recalled, too, the more recent suicide of a ridge resident who chose death at his own hands rather then suffering with cancer.

Bill Sobers' home bears the marks of its earliest years as a log house, and said it actually was built before Monroe

County was carved out of Northampton County. In basement beams are notches he said were used as gun mounts by settlers defending themselves against Indians.

For the purposes of this book, however, it is another home, across the road from Sobers Meat Market, which adds even more to the legend of Suicide Ridge.

For years, Bill Sobers said, the place was known simply as the "haunted house," primarily because of the cryptic ghost which was painted on its mailbox.

As it turns out, the "haunted house" was occupied for many years by none other than Emma Finkbeiner and her husband.

They bought the place because they really did believe it was haunted, and felt there was something charismatic about it. They eventually sold it not because of the rumors that it was haunted, but because of increasing traffic and noise from the adjacent highway.

Before the Sobers put up their meat market across the street, that lot was a popular "lover's lane" for area young people. It was said that ghosts would be seen dancing around.

The Finkbeiners old house, on the edge of Suicide Ridge, has had a checkered past, including many tales of human drama. Unfortunately, this well-known "haunted house" has precious few ghost stories connected to it.

Still, Suicide Ridge remains a frightening place for those who remember the stories and have had their own strange encounters there.

Such is the case with Ralph Meisse, of Sciota, who remembered a brutally cold, moonlit December night several years ago on the old Werkheiser farm, site of the father-son suicide.

Meisse was on the land to, as he put it, "cop a Christmas tree." There was a crusty coating of snow on the ground, and it crunched beneath the soles of their boots as they tramped along the ridge on their larcenous way.

"My buddy, Paul," Meisse began, "was about thirty yards away from me. He was cutting a tree for himself, and I was looking for one for me.

"So he's cutting, and I'm looking for a tree. We hear something coming. There are no houses except the farm house just over the hill.

"We heard this 'crunch-crunch' sound, it sounded like a man walking. It was not a deer. Both of us folded into a tree to hide from whatever it was."

As Ralph and his friend cowered in the protective branches of the a tree, the sound seemed to come closer and closer.

"Whatever it was, it walked right by us, and there was nothing there. Nothing at all. The footsteps were maybe 15, 20 yards away from us. We heard the noise, it came between us. There was the sound of the crunching snow, but when we finally looked, there were no foot prints.

"Whatever it was, it stopped between us for a moment and started to walk again. It walked right over the ridge."

Whether it was the cold of the night or their own fears, the two young men froze for what seemed like an eternity before proceeding back off the ridge.

"But Paul, he wouldn't go back over that ridge ever again," Ralph concluded.

Ralph said it has always seemed that property around Suicide Ridge (or Hanging Ridge or Suicide Road, as variations have it) has been difficult to sell, and many other stories have been told about the area.

Take, for example, the tale of Charlie, a friend of Ralph's. Charlie was repairing the slate roof of a barn in which a man had hanged himself. As he positioned himself near a fairly large hole in the roof, he looked down into the barn to see the hangman's noose still dangling from a rafter.

Shaken by the sight, Charlie began to slide down the slick and steep barn roof.

He might have fallen to his death, had not an unseen force grabbed his leg and saved him.

Such is life, and death, on Suicide Ridge.

THE SWEETHEART OF SIGMA PI

It looms at the top of the hill as an awesome presence. Where Smith and Analomink Streets meet, a couple blocks from the East Stroudsburg University campus, the Sigma Pi fraternity house is positioned on a broad expanse of land which is perfectly suited for the presence of a ghost.

And, as fate would have it, the old house is, in a very real way, haunted.

We met the brothers in the broad parking lot to the rear of the white Victorian house which has served Sigma Pi since the fraternity was established there in 1961.

Quite frankly, at the time of the investigation into the haunting of Sigma Pi, the frat house could have been the setting for the movie "Animal House." Partying obviously took precedent over housekeeping in the cozy confines of the old house.

But we were not there for inspection, we were there to learn more about "Margie," the indefatigable spirit which has made her presence known at Sigma Pi.

We ascended a dark staircase to the third floor, guided there by an accommodating brother who told us not to mind the growling of Pookie, the house dog.

Still, we cautiously sidestepped the mutt and proceeded toward a door marked with a purloined "RESERVED FOR CLERGY" parking sign. As it turns out, behind that sign on the door is the room in which the ghost of Margie is presumed to dwell.

The room is variously called "The Chapel" or "Margie's Room," and once its door was swung open, it became obvious why the former sobriquet has been applied.

Noticeable on a far wall, which becomes the front wall of the house, are colorful stained glass windows.

"So the story goes," began our appointed tour guide, "when the frat took over, that area over there (he pointed to the stained glass windows) was all sealed off, behind a wall. When they started to redo the house, they broke down the wall and found only one thing in that small chamber . . . an urn."

In the urn, it is believed, were the ashes of Margie.

Margie, so the legend goes, was a housekeeper in the big house. It is told that she struck up a love affair with the master of the house, and as the result of the indiscretion, wound up being banished to the third floor room, where it is said she rocked on a chair in disgrace and loneliness until she died in that small room. The story also alleges that after Margie's body was cremated, the urn containing her ashes was placed in the room and the room was then sealed off by the construction of a wall.

"When they were gutting the rooms up there," the young man continued," the urn was knocked over, and the ashes spilled out. They were tearing down that wall, and didn't know what was behind it.

"That was supposedly the beginning of Margie's haunting here. Her ghost is in the house now, and it wanders all over the house. She's all over, and a lot of unexplained things happen all the time."

Two brothers lived in Margie's Room at the time of this writing, and over the years they and others who have preceded them have reported brushes with Margie.

One of them continued: "There's a crawl space above the room, at the peak of the house. One night, one of the guys decided to sleep up there. He woke up and was totally frozen. He couldn't move or talk for about thirty seconds. He felt a terrible pressure on his chest. He claimed Margie was present, and had him in her control.

"Another brother lived in the Red Room upstairs, across the hall from Margie's. He had a similar experience, and he also blamed it on the ghost."

There have been countless other incidents inside the frat house which have been blamed on the ghost. Items have mysteriously fallen to the floor, telephones have rung in strange sequences, and many residents and visitors have reported strange sensations in nearly every room.

Even Pookie has seemed to respond to unseen commands and has growled at thin air.

Margie, the ghost of Sigma Pi, has become well known throughout the ESU campus. The frat brothers capitalize on their haunting when Margie is represented in a "haunted house" fund-raiser at Halloween.

But when the lights go out, the parties wind down (and that isn't often), and things are quiet in the old, nineteenth century house, the ghost of Margie begins to make its presence known.

As one young man says, however, "We feel she protects us, in a way. Nobody's afraid, really. Margie's a good ghost."

THE GHOSTLY LEGIONNAIRE

In the course of seeking out spooks, there are times the search takes unexpected twists and turns.

Take, for example, the morning we walked into the Post Office in Canadensis. We were making "cold calls" across the region, popping in and out of general stores, diners, fire halls and other gathering spots asking locals about any alleged "haunted houses" or ghostly activities in their areas.

Post offices are usually good sources in such situations. Letter carriers get around more than most folks, and if there's a story to be told out there, they're likely to find out somewhere along the line.

In the case at Canadensis, however, the postal workers knew nothing. They were very helpful, and managed to scrounge up an old history book from a dusty shelf in the tiny post office. It was interesting, but provided no ghost leads.

"Oh, you guys should talk to Mary," one worker exclaimed. The others in the room chimed in agreement. Mary, they all said, would know any ghost story about Canadensis, if there were any.

We were preparing to gather the information on how we might contact Mary when, within a few seconds of learning about her and her vast knowledge of the area, she walked through the front door of the post office!

We knew then that it was going to be a good day.

Mary Price-Wicks, it turns out, is a retired postmaster at Canadensis. She is also a keeper of the historic flame thereabouts and, as it turned out, knew a ghost story or two.

She finished her business at the post office and ordered us to follow her out to the hardware store in Mountain Home. There, she told us, we would find Sam Jones. Sam, she assured us, would have a doozy of a ghost story for us.

Moments later, we arrived at Mountain Home and, sure enough, Sam was standing out front. Mary and Sam exchanged morning salutations and introduced us to him.

"Oh, yeah," Sam said, "I have a great story for you."

The encounter resulted in a full morning with Sam, his family and friends, and some of the unseen inhabitants of one of the friendliest areas of the Poconos.

Sam got down to business by setting the stage for a most incredible story.

"We were sitting at the bar of the American Legion hall. Sam Everett was sitting with me that particular evening, but then he moved down the bar a bit.

"Sam kissed all the girls good night and left. Well, shortly after he left, the ash tray in front of me started going back and forth and back and forth, moving about six inches each way. I mean, it wasn't just a little bit, it was really moving!"

Jones admitted that he had had a couple of drinks that night, but not nearly enough for his mind to play those kind of tricks on him.

"This went on for about twenty minutes or so," he continued, "but I didn't want to say anything to anybody, because I didn't want anybody saying I was nuts."

Jones wouldn't have had to worry, however, since it was quickly revealed to him that others in the bar had witnessed the shuffling ashtray. But in a mental Mexican standoff, none told the others.

"The bartender, and another guy saw it, and they didn't want to say anything, either."

The moving ashtray remained a mystery to the men for the rest of the night, and if not for a tragic event, might have confounded them for the rest of their lives. But something happened in the hours which followed the bizarre barside movement that cast a new light on the matter.

Sam Jones grew quite serious as he continued his story.

"We didn't think a whole lot about all of it at the time, but the next morning, we learned that Sam Everett died."

Everett, we remind you, had just left the Legion hall, and had been sitting at the seat in front of the rambling ashtray.

The ashtray incident was just the beginning of a series of strange events which may or may not be blamed on the spirit of Sam Everett.

One episode in particularly baffling, and several Legionnaires will readily confirm its occurrence.

Sam Jones continued his story. "A bunch of guys were playing cards there one night. They had two decks of cards. One was red, one was blue."

Jones measured his words carefully as he detailed the complicated chain of events which followed.

"While they were playing cards with the red deck, the cards turned blue, or vice versa. The cards' colors actually changed. As the cards changed during play, the spare cards did not change."

Jones emphasized that although the prospect of playing cards changing colors in front of the eyes of card players is a bit difficult to fathom, there are several men who will swear to the events.

"As all of this happened," Sam said, "I decided to count the cards. There were 53 in the deck on the table and only 51 in the deck we were playing with. We found the one missing in our deck was the queen of hearts. So we took the queen of hearts from the other deck and put it back into the deck we were using, and John shuffled them, and they turned to red again."

John is John Ranze, a retired man who lives near the Legion hall in Mountain Home. He verified everything Sam Jones said, and added, "Six guys were playing, and there was no trick involved. One guy got so upset he got up and left."

Since the ashtray and playing card incidents, patrons and employees at the Legion hall have tempted whatever energy may be there with "readings" from a Ouija board, and widespread speculation has risen that yes, indeed, the Legion hall is haunted.

"Things get very realistic," Sam Jones continued. "One night, we heard footsteps shuffling across upstairs, and we went up to check, but nobody was there."

THE SNOWY MOUNTAIN GHOST

The afternoon was icy cold and the sky was a steel gray. Driving up Route 191 south of Stroudsburg just hours after a frozen rain mingled with snow coated the road with a perilous glaze may have been foolhardy, but we sensed the journey to Stroudsmoor Country Inn would be worth the risk.

Besides, researching for a ghost book in the Poconos meant traveling on adventurous roads in adverse weather. We were accustomed to taking our time.

In the jargon of the salesman, Stroudsmoor was a "cold call." There was no lead, no idea whatsoever that the place would harbor a ghost, just a hint and a hope.

Spread over 150 acres on a high ridge, broad and brilliant vistas of the town and countryside are provided at Stroudsmoor. The buildings there were known variously as the Highland Inn, Highland Cottage and Ridgecrest. The hillside also was the site of a mine, a busy ice house, and a farm. The hotels were built by Quakers and operated under their strict mores.

The main house at Stroudsmoor serves as a reception area, dining room, lounge and sixteen-room inn. Another former hotel on the grounds, a building said to have been built in the mid-nineteenth century, has been converted into a General Store and gift shop which serves as the centerpiece of the Marketplace, a cluster of country shops located a short walk from the main house and its adjacent cottage.

The setting is quiet and romantic, and the ambience is

that which could be expected in a true family operation.

At Stroudsmoor, it is the Pirone family which keeps a tight rein of quality and satisfaction control over every aspect of their businesses. They took over the Stroudsmoor operation in 1984, and worked very hard to build it into a prosperous venture.

Again, there was no indication at all that there would be supernatural activities at Stroudsmoor. We were really drawn there by the quality of its Victorian-themed and graphically-stunning brochures and handouts. It was obvious in that printed matter that whoever operated this place had a great pride in its heritage and the image it chose to present.

We were not disappointed. The pride was evident, and something else, a bit less evident, was there.

A ghost!

As ghost stories go, the Stroudsmoor General Store ghost, quite frankly, is not movie material. The setting may well be, however.

The old Highland Inn is now an elegant country store. Its manager, Linda Forte (nee Pirone), who also manages The Marketplace, has converted what was the lobby of the old hotel into a well-stocked store. But the most impressive floor of the shop has to be the lower level, which once was the grand ballroom of the Highland.

Not only is the ceiling there covered with intricate Victorian embossed tin, so are the walls. They surround another lovely selection of gift and home decorating items.

Linda is immensely proud of what has been done in what was a fifty-room hotel. And, she had no qualms about discussing the very real probability that at least one ghost haunts it.

The upper floors of the building have been converted into living quarters for the extended Pirone family. More than one person has reported hearing what Linda described as "creaky floors and strange sounds" coming from the third floor in particular. One worker there claims they are the sounds of a spirit.

Linda's sister, Susan Lebel, resides on that floor, and

confirms that there have been creepy moments up there. "I always feel that someone is there," she says, "But I believe they're friendly because people who came there came for vacations, and there were happy times there."

As inconclusive as the ghostly activities in the old hotel may be, the most fetching tale to come out of Stroudsmoor is, as its teller admits, purely fiction. But, it is the kind of enduring ghost story which should be shared with an audience broader than the Pirone children.

Louie Pirone, who bears a striking resemblance to the actor Danny DeVito, is a former educator, aspiring publisher, antiques dealer and raconteur. He is also a masterful storyteller.

With strains of O Solo Mio echoing in the background, we sat with the diminutive Louie Pirone in his antiques-collectible shop, Wibbleton's, in the Marketplace complex.

We had already been assured by other family members that if anyone in their clan could regale us with a ghost story, Louie could.

It is a mythical but magical little story Louie used to tell his children, and their friends, when they gathered together on a cold winter night. The words are Louie's.

"Up here, on top of this mountain, as you get to the top, you'll find a foundation of an old building. There, lives the Snowy Mountain Ghost.

He is a very good ghost, very good. He is actually the helper of Santa Claus in this area. He quietly goes through the mountains and he keeps track of the little children.

"He keeps his records up there, up on Godfrey's Ridge, and when Christmas time comes around, at the beginning of December, he begins to make his reports to Santa.

"If you come up on the ridge and you see the fog on the hill, near the old foundation ruins, the ghost is there, busily compiling the information on which children were good all year, and which were not."

There really is a stone foundation up on Godfrey Ridge, but Louie Pirone freely admits there is little foundation to his story.

"The idea of the story," he says, "is not to frighten children, but to get them to understand that somebody is looking over them to make sure they're being good."

The Pirones have even incorporated the legend of the Snowy Mountain Ghost into their extensive calendar of antique and craft fairs. "A Snowy Mountain Fair" is held yearly on the Sunday following Presidents Day.

If a fog should shroud Godfrey Ridge that day, and Louie Pirone should be in a storytelling mood, the event would not long be forgotten by any child who attends the fair that day.

THE TANNERSVILLE GHOST

Long before Camelback, long before busy Route 611 or even busier I-80, and even before there was a Tannersville, the tiny outpost on the frontier was a strategic and symbolic place.

It was strategic in that General John Sullivan, ordered by the Continental Congress to quell Indian raids in the region, chose the area as an encampment as his troops positioned themselves for the bloody encounters which were to follow.

The Indians of the region had already begun to protect their land and themselves from what they had to consider white invaders.

Under the guidance of the great Berks County Indian negotiator Conrad Weiser, a string of forts had been established along the Pocono Mountain frontier in the 1750s.

The first fort in Monroe Country was erected near the present Shawnee Resort, and another was built in what is now the eastern end of Stroudsburg.

Still another fort was built near what is now Ninth and Main Streets in Stroudsburg. Benjamin Franklin signed the order which established the fort, and Conrad Weiser arranged for the design and manning of the crude, 80-feet square compound. It was named Fort Hamilton, after James Hamilton, who had been a member of the committee appointed by the governor to study security along the frontier in 1775.

In 1763, while he was serving as Pennsylvania's Lieutenant Governor, Hamilton had written to the General Assembly, "I have received well-attested accounts of many barbarous and shocking murders, and other depredations, having been committed by Indians on the inhabitants" of the Pocono Mountains region.

Determined to clear the way for increased settlement of upstate Pennsylvania, the government dispatched Sullivan and what was to become known as "Sullivan's March" was begun.

At what is now the eastern end of Tannersville stood the simple, log structure known as Learned's (or, in some accounts, Larner's, Learn's or Learner's) Tavern.

It was Saturday night, June 19, 1779 when Gen. Sullivan's men set up camp in the forests and clearing near the tavern, while the officers were provided with hospitality in the tavern itself.

The following night, the troops continued their long march north to where the Indians had formed an uneasy and unlikely alliance with Tories and were wreaking havoc on the settlers.

The families which were carving out their homesteads in the wild, vast valley of the Susquehanna had already been beset with troubles, as claims by investors and governments in Pennsylvania and Connecticut both vied for possession of and jurisdiction over the region. They had already girded themselves to withstand possible attacks from the land-grabbers, as the Indians, up to that time, were generally peaceable.

Greatly outnumbered by the incensed Indians and taunting Tories, the able-bodied men and boys of the settlements in the Wyoming Valley hamlets of Plymouth, Nanticoke, Kingston, Wilkes-Barre and Forty Fort were huddled in the blockhouses, hoping to withstand the attacks until help in the form of Gen. Sullivan's troops could arrive.

Historical accounts vary on the activities in the Wyoming Valley in those dark days, but it is generally conceded that the British encouraged the Indians to attack the colonial settlers with various incentives, and the Indians were quick to respond. They had already been fired by the unscrupulous action of the Walking Purchase, which had cheated the natives out of much of their land.

Also quick to respond was the colonial government. Gen. George Washington sent Gen. Sullivan into the dense and largely unexplored wilderness of the Poconos from Easton, through the Wind Gap and onto Wilkes-Barre.

The response was in direct action to a July 3, 1778, massacre near Wilkes-Barre in which 400 settlers were brutally killed by the Indians and Tories.

Ironically, it was a by-product of this conflict which helped in the eventual development of the Pocono region.

A crude path had been cut from Easton northward in the early 1760s, but the need to move a large number of armed forces through the trees gave rise to the opening of a wider swath, which ultimately was to become known as the Sullivan Road.

The troop movements and road-building efforts at the time were complex. It was reported by engineers, surveyors and troop commanders that beyond Learn's Tavern, conditions were virtually impassable.

Thick stands of mountain laurel, crowded woods and random, large swamplands provided many challenges, but by the summer of 1779, a serviceable roadway had been established, and Gen. Sullivan's troops could proceed.

Throughout the Poconos are ancient historical markers which trace the route of the Sullivan Expedition. Near Pocono Pines is "Hungry Hill," where a force of about 500 roadbuilders camped for more than a week.

"Chowder Camp," located between Tannersville and Pocono Pines, was so named by Gen. Sullivan because of the trout and rattlesnake caught and consumed there during his troops march.

At Sciota is Brinker's Mill, which was where the Sullivan army gathered supplies and had breakfast before proceeding to Tannersville.

Letters from soldiers who were part of the Sullivan Expedition detailed what were called amazingly tall trees, wild beasts of all sort, and, what Lt. Col. Henry Dearborn described as "a horrid, rough, gloomy country" which was better known as the Great Swamp.

Dearborn, who would later be appointed Secretary of War, called the gloomiest, thickest part of the swamp, the "Shades of Death."

The phrase has taken on a double meaning among Pocono historians. As the northbound roadbuilders and soldiers found the Great Swamp an unexpected and formidable barrier in their progress, the "Shades of Death" swamp was an even more horrid place for the refugees from the Wyoming Valley massacre.

Hundreds of people, mostly women, children and older men, had fled from their fields and farms as the stronger, younger, men fought in vain to save their homes from the marauders. By the time the refugees reached safety in the forts at what is now Stroudsburg, there were many tales of death and misery in the dense forests and deadly swamp which Lt. Col. Dearborn had so aptly named.

The Sullivan Expedition certainly played a major role in the history and development of the northeastern corner of Pennsylvania, but in a broader historical sense, its implications within the time period of America's frontier expansion and Revolutionary War make it a major campaign in the history of the entire nation.

All of this, of course, has little to do with ghosts.

Or does it?

Tannersville, named for not a person but for an industry, has obviously been a pivotal location in the Poconos.

Then, it was a way station for stage coaches and, indeed, armies. Now, it is the seat of much commerce and business, and well-known to vacationers, diners and shoppers.

Then and now, the Tannersville Hotel has been the centerpiece of activity in the village.

In 1831, a log tavern was located on the site of the present Tannersville Hotel. By 1847, a large hotel was set on 98 acres along the original Scranton to Philadelphia stage coach road. At the time, it was called Miller's Tannersville Hotel, after its owner, Mannasah Miller.

As the horseless carriage became a more efficient mode of transportation, more efficient roads were needed for the increased, heavier traffic. What is now Route 611 bypassed the front entrance of the old hotel, and what was the front of the place became the rear.

Steve Jakubowitz, who purchased the hotel in 1970, is proud of what is one of the most historic inns in Monroe County, and has developed it into one of the most successful and popular restaurants and night spots in the Poconos.

It is also quite haunted.

Steve fondly recalls the history of his pride and joy. He numbers Manassah Miller among his heroes in life, and tells stories about the cattle drives which once took place on the old road in front of the hotel, the carriage houses which once stood on the grounds, and how Mr. Miller, who lived to be 87, repaired harnesses when he wasn't keeping the inn.

To achieve the pleasant blend of quaintness and chic the Tannersville Hotel now enjoys, there was much renovation and construction needed.

"Somebody told us that when the construction began," Steve says, "we may have unearthed or disturbed something here, and that could explain the presence of a ghost or two here."

Steve remembers an incident in his hotel when the unseen being first made itself known.

"After the first construction here, there were a couple of waitresses who worked here at night. When they were closing the room down and they were alone, more than once they felt a presence of someone in the room. It was to the point that they'd turn around and say hello to someone and there would be nobody there.

"And then, the candles would flicker as if somebody was walking through. Sometimes candles would go out, and there'd be no breeze. Candles inside globes would even blow out on their own."

The waitresses have come to call the spirit "Mabel," and feel it is very real, and may be the ghost of a former owner.

While Mabel seems to inhabit the dining rooms of the main floor, another unidentified phantom may reside on the second floor.

"More than once," Steve admits, "I have awakened in the middle of the night and felt a presence in my bedroom.

"I've never actually seen an apparition, exactly, but I can sense a swirling energy of motion. As I would look into the room from my bed, I would see this smoky energy swirling, and feel it, too. The hair on the back of my neck would stand up. I wouldn't be afraid, because I known enough about this to know there is nothing to be afraid of. My brother has felt much the same energy, and so have others who have spent any time in the room."

Steve remembers even more episodes upstairs. "There was one man who boarded in another room, and he said he once saw the ghost of a young man standing at the foot of his bed," he says.

"Another gent, a character who worked for us awhile and used to hike the Appalachian Trail, also saw a figure at the foot of his bed up here. He said it was the ghost of a young, black man," Steve concludes.

Indeed, and with all due respect to the dear, departed Mabel and the other ghost upstairs, it may well be the ghostly energy of that young black man which is dominant at the Tannersville Inn.

Unbeknownst to Steve, a medium was brought to enjoy a dinner at the inn. Working, one might say, under cover, the medium was asked to silently and unobtrusively "read" the old hotel and provide, if she could, some clues as to if, and how, the place is haunted.

Uncomfortable as she was with the "sneak" reading, she obliged and was taken with the strength of the energy in the old entrance lobby on Learn Road.

It can be asserted that the medium had no knowledge of any past or present historical or supernatural events which had taken place in or near the inn. But it is interesting to note her almost immediate response to the place.

"I feel anguish, pain . . . and, I don't want to say this, but . . . death. It wasn't here, exactly, not this pain, but somewhere very close." She spoke as we walked along the roadway from the parking space into the inn.

"I sense screams, maybe crying, maybe, yes, howling of some sort," she continued. There is smoke and there is blood . . . much blood, this is all I sense, but it is very strong, very close to this spot."

It is interesting to note that history has recorded a 1781 massacre of the Learn family by natives. The family's cabin was close to the site of the Tannersville Inn.

Once inside the inn, the medium cast her eyes skyward and shuddered as a more powerful energy consumed her.

There was no show, no scene. Anyone who may have noticed her actions would have thought she was shaking off a chill on what was an icy evening.

"Oh, yes, there is a very strong energy here," she stated, almost with glee. "I feel that a horse, and maybe more than one horse, plays a role here. Is it? Yes it is, a very bad accident. It was an accident with two horses, I believe, and a carriage, a black cab, I think they called it. They were young, I mean, the people in the cab were young."

What reads as the flight of thought are the exact words of the medium, who wishes to remain anonymous. She seemed to become more and more engrossed in the story which was unfolding through the shards of information she was receiving through whatever psychic means she employed.

"Two of them, and there were three, two of them walked away. These are the people, I mean. I think, but I cannot be sure, that one of the horses had to be destroyed. I think it was, maybe somewhere around 140 years ago or somewhere near there.

"The energy seems to swirl, or spiral, from upstairs. An upstairs room is where the energy is strongest."

All of this took place in an almost whispering tone as we walked slowly from the entranceway into the main dining room.

"Yes, I know it now. It is a black man, a young black man. I feel that he was the driver. It was he, and this I am nearly certain, who did not survive the accident. I believe he was crushed by a falling horse as he fell from his carriage seat. It was terrible, and he died either out there or in here. It is his ghost here, a young, black man. And there may be others."

With that hushed, but chilling account out of the way, the medium and the writer proceeded calmly to a table and a fine meal.

A POCONO POLTERGEIST

This is a strange one. It will probably be the strangest, most incomprehensible and, perhaps, the most frightening story you will read in this book.

It is most frightening because it is quite contemporary, quite real and the reverberations from it continue to dwell in the minds and the innermost psyches of all who were involved.

It took place not on a windy, remote Pocono mountain-top, under a full moon, or in the nineteenth century. It took place on a weekend in February, 1983, on a quiet residential street in Stroudsburg.

It is a modern folktale. It is a legend in the making.

Those who lived through the incident are still very much alive, and many are very willing to discuss what may or may not have happened.

As this is basically a book of ghost stories, it is stretching that premise a tad when this story is presented. We offer it only in whatever context you choose to accept it, and trust you, as a reader, will be as fascinated as it we, the authors, were when we pieced it all together.

Legally, morally and ethically, the story treads on dangerous grounds. Thus, to protect the properties and people involved in the incident, all names except for those of certain individuals who investigated the bizarre events and granted permission to use their names and positions.

To the time of this writing, there are those who had direct knowledge of what happened that winter weekend who prefer not to discuss the matter. Although officers from the Stroudsburg Police Department were on the scene of the episode, the hierarchy in the department has made every attempt to stifle any research into the matter.

The Pocono Record made note of the occurrence, back in 1983, but it could not be very specific. "Monroe County authorities are checking, if somewhat casually, into reports of unexplained phenomena . . .," wrote reporter Kevin McCaney. He continued, "The events that have drawn attention, and fueled varying and fantastic rumors around the town . . . have concerned mostly the appearance of water from unexplained sources and sudden changes in room temperatures, though none have been confirmed by authorities."

The story alluded to the rapid-fire rumors which gripped many people in Stroudsburg. "Though stories about what happened are widespread on the street," McCaney wrote, "most have been embellished, some greatly, and none of the happenings have been confirmed by an authoritative source."

What follows is a series of interviews and transcripts from what could be considered "authoritative sources." One of the individuals is a respected investigator of psychic and unusual phenomena. Another is a photographer and parapsychic who was among the first on the scene of the incident.

Finally, our authoritative sources include the young man who was the source of the monstrous events and the owner of the home in which they took place.

Chip Decker, an art education graduate from Penn State University and a professional photographer by trade, is also a parapsychic and a member of the Pennsylvania Association for the Study of the Unexplained (PASU).

Through Decker are funneled various reports of Unidentified Flying Objects, strange creatures, ghosts and poltergeistic activities.

The latter category is what brought him to the Stroudsburg home after the events of February 26 and 27, 1983.

Decker says the Stroudsburg Police had already been

on the case for two days when he was called in to assess the situation.

One police officer, who has since departed the Stroudsburg force, showed up at Decker's door, urging him to go to the affected home and photograph things which would "knock his socks off." The officer had been one of at least three policemen who had been on the scene that weekend.

Aware that Decker was a parapsychic, the police officer also asked if there was anything which could be done to ward off any evil forces which may be involved in the happenings inside the home.

His curiosity piqued, Decker offered flimsy advice, but hastened to organize a quick response to the officer's nervous quest.

He made a call to his friend and renowned psychic investigator Stan Gordon, in Greensburg, Pa. Gordon was director of PASU. After hearing the initial reports of what was going on in the Stroudsburg house, Gordon advised Decker not to become involved.

He suggested that experienced demonologists be called in. Two specific investigators in that field were recommended, but were unavailable at that time.

Instead, Decker assembled all the principals in the matter inside the two-story single home near the center of town.

About a dozen people gathered in the living room of the house. Decker remembers that a fire was blazing in the fireplace, but the room still felt damp and cold.

Decker was at once impressed and somewhat distressed by what transpired in the course of his interview with those who were directly involved.

"It was a typical poltergeist case," he affirms. "It was not a hoax, simple because there were too many people involved."

He continued, "In my personal opinion, I don't think there was a single person in that house who was not telling me the truth. I believe they saw what they saw, and they're not making anything up. And they were not, underline not, exaggerating. They were very calm, but very scared."

What happened there is a very complex, sometimes confusing chain of events which may make the skeptical even more skeptical, or have the total opposite effect.

To set the stage for the actual details, let us call our central characters Joan and Dennis.

Dennis was the 21-year old man who had recently been released from the Monroe County Prison after doing time for a burglary conviction.

He was alone and shuffling between the streets and Salvation Army shelter in Stroudsburg in the winter of 1982–83 when he was befriended by Joan and her family.

Dennis was taken in by Joan's family, and when he arrived there, so did the family's unspeakable horrors.

The young man's ability to perceive what was happening to him and to those around him may have been diminished by various factors in his background, but in subsequent, separate interviews with him and others who witnessed events, the stories were consistent and corroborative.

Joan provided the most riveting of that testimony. The following are direct quotes from an extensive tape recorded interview conducted by author researcher, Peter Jordan.

Jordan, a New Jersey-based investigator of paranormal phenomena with a masters in psychology, was assigned the Stroudsburg case by Gordon of PASU after Chip Decker's initial contact.

The first question Jordan asked the woman was the most obvious: How and when did everything begin?

It was early in the evening on Saturday night when, as Joan said with a deceiving innocence, "It started raining."

Mind you, outside the house, everything was quite dry. It was raining inside the house. In the living room.

The harrowing experience had begun.

What's more, it was not a rainfall in a traditional sense. It was a fierce storm of wetness.

"Once in a while," Joan said, "you would see it flying in front of you. I mean it would come off the wall. My husband had bent over like this and he was putting a cigarette out and it came up off the floor and smacked him right in the face."

Joan explained that "it" was an alternately cold and warm liquid which could be either clear or a reddish brown color. "And," she continued, "it was a real sticky, just sticky feeling."

A Stroudsburg police officer who asked his name not be used later confirmed to the authors that he remembered the liquid to be a light oily substance. In fact, as he was on the job, investigating the incident, the substance hit his (and other officers') leather uniform coats. He said the liquid seemed to defy the natural flow of gravity and flow or roll upward on their coats.

Chip Decker's probe also determined that the "rain" was actually an oily liquid which sprayed from the walls of the home as if being shot from powerful water pistols.

As this almost unbelievable episode played out, and a family watched in bewildered fear, Dennis became the focus of attention for the half-dozen people in the room at the time.

Joan continued. "Dennis went upstairs to the bathroom," she said. "He came downstairs and he was shaking like a leaf and my husband said, 'what's wrong with you?', and Denny says, 'I think I'm going crazy.' And here his arms had, well, claw marks is all I can say. It was just claw marks going up his arm. Tore it open."

Joan said there was blood coming from the gashes, and Denny was visibly shaken.

Of course, Joan had her suspicions on how the cuts could have been made, fearing they may have been self-inflicted. She asked Denny what had happened.

In separate testimony, Dennis told Pete Jordan about that particular incident. "I had just got done on the toilet and I got up and all the lights were off except the bathroom light and I turned off the light," he said. "I didn't feel anybody hit me or push me or anything, I just felt like a cold flash. And when I got downstairs, I stopped there at the bottom of the step and I had my sleeves rolled up and I looked at my arms."

His arms were scratched and bleeding. He had no idea why.

He continued his recollections of the incident. "I pulled the sleeves down and I just sat on the couch. I guess I was staring off in space 'cause Joan asked me what happened and I didn't say anything."

Meanwhile, Joan likened the gashes to "what would come from a cat."

As Denny reckoned with his strange misfortune, a damp coldness enveloped those in the room. Even though, as Joan recalled, the heater was on full-blast, the coldness persisted and the "rain" kept falling.

"That was a constant," Joan said. "It was constant until Sunday morning. Then it stopped."

But that Saturday night in that Stroudsburg home would never be forgotten by anyone involved.

While he has looked into countless reports of the extraordinary, even the intrepid and generally unshakable Chip Decker still finds this particular case difficult to discuss.

"I am haunted by it," he says. "I'm glad for the experience, but it haunts me. It's like a never-ending story."

And what you have read was only the relatively tame beginning of what was to follow. Joan remembers that the water oozed or shot out of the walls throughout the night. It was about three o'clock in the morning when, faced with something she could not deal with, Joan sought solace by reading the Bible.

"I was reading the 91st psalm," she said, "and my face was drenched. It was dripping off my face. Not one drop touched the Bible, but my face was soaking wet.

"It was just hitting me. I had no fear the whole time, I had no fear at all . . . until I saw the attack."

The "attack" Joan referred to defied all reason.

Dennis was in an upstairs room when, in his own words, "All of a sudden it was cold . . . and as best I can remember, I came up off the floor, at least twelve inches."

He said it did not feel as if he was being physically lifted by anyone or anything, but remembered a shuddering sensation. "It felt like being in a thunder and lightning

81

storm at night and you can feel the electricity in the air, sort of tingling. That's how it felt."

The feeling took control of his entire body, and he swore that for what couldn't have been more than three seconds or so, he was lifted at least a foot off the floor.

Joan's husband was with Dennis at the time, and he confirmed to Joan that, in her recollection, he "heard a whack and he looked up and he saw Denny's head fly backwards and at the same time his body lifted up in the air and just slammed down to the floor."

Dennis fell to the floor with a thud, and others in the house rushed upstairs to see what had happened. He screamed, and an unseen force slashed his face.

"It tore his neck open," said Joan.

Dennis said Joan ran upstairs, and with her husband, took hold of him and dragged him down the stairs. The "rain" was continuing, and the mystery was widening.

As Joan said, "and then it went nuts, the whole house went nuts."

Throughout Saturday night, the water continued to spray from the walls, and everyone tried in vain to get some rest.

By Sunday morning, Joan decided to square off against whatever force was tormenting her family. "I decided, like a ninny, I was going to scrub this thing out of my house. I mean, I just tore the whole living room apart and the dining room and I scrubbed walls. I scrubbed floors and I'll be honest with you, if there was water flying I didn't notice because I was just, I had to do something. But the minute I sat down and rested, then the water started."

The liquid seemed to rise from the floor, and drenched almost every piece of furniture.

With that, one of the women in the room said she had had enough. She demanded a "sign" from whatever or whoever was causing the anguish. "All of a sudden," Joan said, "the whole house was filled with the smell of burning wood."

If anything, the woman's call for a sign seemed to intensify the attacks.

Dennis was victimized once again. He recalled, "All of a sudden I felt something burning on my chest. I looked down and it was this Cross. I hurried up and took the Cross off my head and threw it to the floor. Joan said I shouldn't do that and went to pick it up and she threw it to the floor, too."

The Cross was on a gold necklace Dennis was wearing at the time, and when Pete Jordan interviewed him, the Cross still bore scorch marks Dennis claimed were the result of the incident that Saturday night.

One of the most gruesome circumstances to take place that weekend was when Dennis was overtaken by the invisible force and his body became totally distorted.

Joan tried to describe Denny's appearance. "His arms were drawn up . . . his neck was twisting . . . and all of a sudden, his torso just, well, it went around. It was something I never want to see again."

Dennis said it was very painful. "It was like cold electricity," he said, as he explained how his entire body twisted and contorted in a paralyzing, ungodly position.

Joan said, "I figured the only thing to beat this thing would be love, and we just wrapped our arms around Denny and all of a sudden he just went limp and out cold. He passed out."

Dennis remembered things a bit differently. While Joan credited "love," as the force that relieved him of his agony, Dennis recalled that her husband, "got mad and started cussing it, the spirit or something, then all of a sudden it just let go." Love or cussing, it didn't matter. The force was broken, at least for the time being.

The family didn't have much time to breathe easily after that attack, because soon after, as Dennis said, "things started to happen stronger" by Sunday night.

By that time, the pool of those who had become involved in some way spread to members of the Stroudsburg Police Department and the local clergy. The police became involved when one officer responded mid-morning on Sunday, offered some advice on how to combat the force with Rosary beads and Holy Water, and promised to return later.

Joan said there were four police officers on the scene Sunday night, and the liquid began to spray once again, intensifying as it pelted the officers' leather coats.

Following several incidents Sunday afternoon, four police officers arrived early that evening. According to Joan, they seemed to have a predisposition that Dennis was manipulating the people and manufacturing the "rain," the contortion, the levitation and everything else.

"They even called the police chief in, and he no sooner got in the door when he got smacked right in the face with the water," Joan recalled.

Dennis said they as much as told him they believed the "rain" in the house was caused by Dennis spitting.

The officers instructed Dennis to accompany them upstairs. "They were playing games," Joan says. "The minute I saw Denny go up the steps with my husband behind him I said no, don't do that, because I just had a gut feeling that the kid was going to get hurt again."

Dennis continues his own recollections of his meeting with the police. "We went upstairs and one officer says to go get a paper bag. So they bring a paper bad and told me to stick it over my head."

The police were testing their "spitting" theory through what one of them called a "process of elimination."

Dennis claims their experiment failed. "They went right behind me with the paper bag over my head and they were still getting wet. The bag wasn't wet. There was no indication I was spitting. Then (one of the officers) said 'hold these,' and he put in my hand Rosary Beads that were blessed. So I am standing there for about two minutes with a paper bag over my head and it was still raining. Then all of a sudden my hands got very warm. It didn't get too hot, but it got very warm. I threw down the Rosary Beads and as soon as I did, I got pushed. This time, literally pushed. It was like someone went behind me and all over my body pushed and I fell right at the officers' feet. I wasn't levitated this time, just pushed."

Things got worse. "The left side of my face felt like somebody took needles and just stabbed me in the face. I let out a bellow and they all turned on the lights. And then they took off the paper bag and I was scratched."

Dennis said the policemen examined him, and found blood throughout the inside of the paper bag. "Then," he continued, "(one of the officers) left the room, went down the stairs and outside."

That officer, who did not want his name mentioned, did later confirm that he left the scene in haste.

Joan did concede that one of the officers offered some comfort. He provided Chip Decker's contact number, and seemed to be genuinely concerned about the family's plight.

Even members of the local clergy were summoned in an attempt to sort out what was happening at the Stroudsburg home that weekend.

A Catholic priest refused to perform an exorcism, and wouldn't even visit the afflicted family.

But a Methodist minister and an associate did respond to Joan's frantic call for spiritual guidance. She remembered the greeting they received: "This was about 2:30 Sunday night," she said.

"Denny had fallen asleep on the couch, but it was a restless sleep. He was dreaming and shaking real bad. It was almost like convulsive, like shaking. And they did come and they prayed and they laid their hands on him and prayed. All of a sudden, it was like a miracle. The whole house warmed up. I mean, the house got warm.

"This yukky odor left and Denny woke up and it was like nothing had ever happened. Nothing has happened since then. Absolutely nothing.

In all, the events in the Stroudsburg home remain baffling to both the family members who say they lived them and the investigators who probed them.

In many ways, it is the stuff of a classic encounter with a poltergeist. Kitchen implements rattled, water seemingly seeped from walls.

It is a ghost story of a sort. Silent shadows were seen, an upstairs chair levitated. A little girl in the house claimed to see a fluorescent green glow in the shape of a human in a corner of the darkened kitchen, its eye sockets merely vacant cavities.

Police officers who were willing to talk remain ambivalent. They will not deny that what they witnessed was confusing and bizarre, but in their jobs, they see much of which is unexplainable. "But not that kind of stuff," confided one of them.

As for the investigators Pete Jordan and Chip Decker, the story is, in a sense, almost too good not to be true. Intense interviews with the principals were tidy and consistent, and many of the particulars are compatible with those in similar cases of "possession" and/or poltergeist activity.

Was it a hoax? Peter Jordan says no. "Absolutely not," he affirms. "I thought so when I first got involved, and I'm kind of a skeptical investigator myself. My background's pretty analytical (with an M.S. in psychology), and more often than not, these things turn out to be nothing more than folklore."

Was it a cheap attempt at notoriety, publicity, or some bizarre sense of fame? "No," reiterates Jordan. "This thing is legitimate. The reason I believe that is that the police officers I spoke to were convinced it was really happening, and nobody was clambering for any publicity."

Most of all, was it frightening to those who spent that harrowing weekend (the weekend of a full moon, we might add) in that Stroudsburg house?

"Oh, yes," said Joan, "it was very scary."

But it is over now. Dennis has moved on, and there were further stories of similar activities whirling around him as this book was being written. That house was not haunted, in the classic sense, and this story was thus not a ghost story. But, as an appropriate ending for what we hope has been a thought-provoking and entertaining book, reflect for a few minutes on what you have just read . . . sleep tight tonight!

CONCLUSION

What is interesting about publishing a first book of ghost stories in any particular area is that many of the best tales do not emerge until after the book is in the hand of readers.

Only then do those who were not ferreted out during the exhaustive research period realize that someone out there was indeed collecting ghost stories. The telephone calls and letters begin to pour in, each with something like "I read your book and enjoyed it, but you should hear what happened to me!"

The authors truly hope this will happen after "Pocono Ghosts" hits the stores. A second volume of ghost stories, legends and tales of the unexplained in the Poconos, most notably in the northern section, is already in the works, and any contributions or leads will be appreciated.

Within the time restraints of the research phase for this book, many tips and potential tales were left untracked and some stories were thus left to be sorely lacking in details and depth.

This, of course, can be expected, considering the nature of the stories being collected. Those who have experienced brushes with the unknown are often befuddled by what has taken place.

Witness Bob Pivak, a Canadensis-area baker and artist who is at wit's end to figure out exactly what has gone on in the pleasant rural rental house he shares with his wife.

Bob's art is in the carving of slate, stone and wood. He admits to being quite meticulous when it comes to his carving tools. He knows where they are, all the time. That is, unless the ghost he believes haunts his home has other ideas.

Chisels disappear, water leaks where there is no water appear, ceiling panels drop, eerie "whooshing" sounds are heard, and things go ding in the night.

Oh, yes, things have gone "bump" in the night there, too. But it is the nocturnal "dings" that frustrate Bob. One of Bob's passions is bells, and he has a lot of them. Some, to his bewilderment, have chimed completely on their own.

There have been many renovations done to the house, and Bob is firmly convinced the remodeling freed the spirit energy in the house. As he carves, it is not unusual for him to feel there is somebody looking over his shoulder.

He would like to think it is the spirit of an old friend, Rusty, who died in an automobile accident several years ago. Rusty was quite the prankster, Bob recalls, and maybe he has returned to play a few more jokes on his old friend.

Down in Wind Gap, Dolores Klingel says she's "fascinated" by the lights that go on and off about five or six times a night in her apartment above an old movie house.

Dolores and her daughter, Christine Nordmark, have both experienced one or more of the phenomena on one or more occasions. Puddles of water show up on the kitchen floor, despite no visible leaks anywhere. Any from time to time, Dolores feels the very clear (and very disconcerting) sensation of someone gently touching her wrist.

"I'm not afraid," she says, "I'm fascinated."

Fascinated as well is the owner of the El Coyote restaurant and night club at the crossroads of Routes 715 and 314 in Meisertown.

Rumors circulate around the area that ghosts ramble around the old inn and its grounds, and its proprietor isn't quick to disagree.

"A man owned the place, and I never really found out what he did, but it's said he was lynched on a tree out back. I don't really know what tree it is, either. But the story goes that his brother, who had come in to settle the estate, was later found hanged on the same tree."

What is now a Mexican-flavored roadhouse was built sometime before the Civil War, and was used as a meeting house for a religious congregation. More recently, it was the "Club Alpine" square-dance hall.

Are there ghosts in El Coyote? "I don't know," she says, but I think I'm kind of susceptible to believing in those sort of things. And yes, we kind of feel things around here."

"The people who used to live upstairs here had things happen. His girlfriend said that one night she felt the presence of a little girl brush past her face. She looked as she felt the sensation, and saw the form of a little girl standing there in a robe. She did have a real daughter, and she rushed into her room to check on her. Her little girl was sound asleep, and her robe was hanging from a hook on her closet door.

One of the oldest roadside hotels in the Poconos is the Swiftwater Inn. For as long as anyone can remember, perhaps since its establishment in 1778, there has been a sign at the Swiftwater with the comforting message, "Rest ye Bones, Tickle ye Palate and Nae Rob ye Wallet." The motto is testimony to the relaxed ambience, good meals and reasonable prices there. And what's more, the Swiftwater Inn is apparently haunted, but Joan Cooper wants nothing of that notion.

Joan, who has owned the inn since 1973, operates it with the help of her two adult daughters. And while none of them has seen or experienced anything there, one incident in the 1980s confirmed there was something supernatural going on within its walls.

The occasion was a gathering of psychics who, for a reason unknown to Joan Cooper, chose the Swiftwater Inn as a site for a seance and psychic "sleepover." As they grouped together to "read" the energy inside the inn, they formed a circle and immediately had "vibes" that there was spectral activity in the room.

"When they had that seance," she said, "the people

running it lost control and someone from the circle had to come out of it and help another one. And then, everybody just flew out of here that night. Nobody stopped."

Joan was frightened. "It was more than a trance," she said. One person came out speaking another language! I never had another one again. No, not from that reaction. It was bad.

"They said they saw spirits," she concluded, "but they said they were scared to death."

That was enough for Joan to hear to know she would rather not delve any deeper into the psychic energy of the Swiftwater Inn.

Down in the rugged Minisink Hills, in the crotch of Brodhead Creek and the Delaware River, is the rustic Minisink Hotel.

In his eloquent history of the old hotel, noted Poconos historian Bob Brooks recalled the time when on the same site was once a grain storage shed associated with the general store and grist mill of Benjamin Shoemaker. This mid-eighteenth century venture grew into a tavern, stage coach shop and inn, and has prospered ever since.

Brooks intimated, with his literary tongue firmly planted in his historical cheek, "On dark, still, moonless nights, Ann Shoemaker's ghost may still bang on a washtub with a wooden spoon to warn Daniel and Benjamin working their fields along Brodhead Creek. For, the Indian presence still lurks between Church and Zimmerman Hills, within the gurgling of Marshall's Creek, inside the very walls of Minisink Hotel."

While the present owners of the hotel could recall no ghostly events in their establishment, it was within those walls that Rick Strunk, a familiar face there, revealed the details of a presence which has resided in his house for several years.

As a handful of barside patrons listened in, Rick told of a pathetic spirit of a woman who lived and died in his Hillside Drive home. He calls her Molly.

When his own child was a baby, Rick said, he would notice a rocking chair slowly moving back and forth in one corner of his living room. "People tell me I'm nuts," he said, "but I know she's there. Molly was a woman who died in the house.

"Before I moved into that home, back in about 1980, if someone would have told me about any ghosts, I would have told them they were nuts, too. But now I believe."

Rick believes that Molly eternally rocks her own baby in that living room chair. "Molly has stood over me many times," he continued. "She has walked into my bedroom a hundred times.

"Molly doesn't make any sound when she moves around, but I know she's there," Rick concluded.

Any college or university worth its salt has its share of ghosts, and East Stroudsburg University is no exception.

While some students make vague mention of spirit activity (that's spirit as in ghost) in the towering Hawthorn Residence Hall on campus, a source no less authoritative than the campus police department openly discusses strange happenings inside the E.S.U. Auditorium on College Circle.

Nobody is quite certain whose ghost might provide the chills inside the stately structure, but it is interesting to know that music legend Fred Waring and his Pennsylvanians once performed there.

While the police officer who reviewed the reports of the auditorium mysteries prefers to remain anonymous, he said students have often reported odd aromas, icy breezes, displaced items and disembodied conversations inside the building.

Other strange events at the Fine and Performing Arts Center on the University campus have been blamed on a feisty phantom who repeatedly alters name plaques on doors and moves paintings out of kilter.

But as you have read in the preceding pages, there are much more substantive stories of ghosts in the charmed Pocono Mountains.

Some people are quick to deny their existence, and this is quite understandable. Others, however, follow a more adventurous course as they walk head-on into the world of the unknown.

The authors thank all of those who came forth with their stories, and those who chose to add this book to their shelves. There is much more of the Poconos to be covered out there. Ghostly activity is known in towns, villages, hills and valleys from Jim Thorpe to Hawley, Metamoras to Moscow.

If you have had an experience, or know of a place in which things indeed "go bump in the night," drop a line to the authors at Exeter House Books, P.O. Box 8134, Reading, Pa. 19601.

ABOUT THE AUTHORS AND ARTIST

David J. Seibold, an avid scuba diver and fisherman, splits his time between homes in Reading, Pa. and Barnegat Light, N.J.

A graduate of Penn State, Seibold is a member of the Barnegat Light Scuba and Rescue Team and operates his own charter boat out of Barnegat Light.

He is a former commodore of the Rajah Temple Yacht Club and is a decorated Vietnam Campaign veteran.

Seibold is employed as senior account executive at radio station WEEU in Reading, and is active in many civic and social organizations.

Charles J. Adams III has written numerous articles, songs and stories, and has authored three books on ghost stories in his native Berks County, as well as seven books on ghosts and shipwrecks with Seibold.

He is a morning radio personality at WEEU radio in Reading, and is the Reading Eagle newspaper's chief travel correspondent.

Adams is a past president of the Reading Public Library and also sits on the executive council and editorial board of the Historical Society of Berks County. He is also a member of the board of directors of the Penn State Alumni Society of the Berks Campus, and several other community groups in Berks County. He is also listed in "Who's Who in Entertainment."

Charles J. Adams Jr., a retired Reading dry cleaning executive, is an accomplished cartoonist and artist, and has been active in community affairs in Reading and Berks County.

ACKNOWLEDGMENTS

The authors wish to recognize and thank the many people, publications and organizations, without whose help, guidance and cooperation, this book would not have been possible.

BOOKS

JOURNEY BY LAMPLIGHT, by Peggy Bancroft, Gun-Ni-At Publishing Co., South Sterling, Pa., 1979.

RINGING AXES AND ROCKING CHAIRS, by Peggy Bancroft, Barrett Friendly Library, 1974.

THE POCONOS, by Carroll B. Tyson, Innes & Sons, Philadelphia, Pa., 1929.

OLD TRAILS AND ROADS IN PENN'S LAND, by John T. Faris, J. B. Lippincott Company, Philadelphia, Pa., 1927.

SEEING PENNSYLVANIA, by John T. Faris, J. P. Lippincott Company, Philadelphia, 1919.

PENNSYLVANIA SONGS AND LEGENDS, George Korson, Editor; The Johns Hopkins Press, Baltimore, Md., 1949.

INDIAN HISTORY AND LEGENDS OF PENNSYL- VANIA'S PICTURESQUE PLAYGROUND, by A. F. Stokes, A. B. Wyckoff, Stroudsburg, Pa.

DELAWARE WATER GAP: ITS SCENERY, ITS LEGENDS AND EARLY HISTORY, by L. W. Brodhead; Sherman and Co., Philadelphia, 1870.

MAGAZINES

This Week in the Poconos
Pennsylvania Heritage
Pennsylvania Folklife

LIBRARIES & ORGANIZATIONS

Kemp Library, East Stroudsburg Univ.; Monroe County
Historical Society; Monroe County Public Library; Pocono
Mountains Vacation Bureau; Delaware Water Gap Natl.
Rec. Area; The Critics' Choice Book Gallery

NEWSPAPERS

The Pocono Record, Reading Eagle, The Mountain Mail,
News of the Poconos

POCONO GHOSTS, LEGENDS AND LORE

DAVID J. SEIBOLD &
CHARLES J. ADAMS III

PHOTO
GALLERY

JAKE

CJA Jr

Margie, the legendary ghost of the Sigma Pi fraternity house in East Stroudsburg, has pested several generations of brothers at this Smith and Analomink Sts. house.

Mesingw, the supernatural being of the forest of Indian lore, is represented in this display at the Pocono Indian Museum.

Does a ghost, or ghosts, walk the ancient floors of historic Fort Depuy in Shawnee?

Eerie music and strange sights are common in the former hotel (left) in the hamlet of Merwinsburg.

Several spirits are said to inhabit the charming Inn at Tannersville.

A family in this home in Sciota has been tormented with ghostly happenings for several years.

They call the ghost of this East Stroudsburg house "Beattie," and she has been noticed by several residents over the years.

An excellent museum and lively ski shop, the Pocono Indian Museum in Marshalls Creek is also home to a lively ghost.

This desk at the International Eatery in Bartonsville, may be the source of the spirit in the popular restaurant along Route 611.

The historic buildings at Stroudsmoor, south of Stroudsburg, harbor many mysteries within their walls.

Does a phantom lurk on the summit of Snowy Hill, south of Stroudsburg?

Many strange tales have come from within the walls of the foreboding old Henryville Inn.

Are these the ruins of a castle built as a haven for Marie Antoinette? It is one of the legends hidden deep in the forests of the Poconos.

The ghost of "Mrs. Booth" has been noticed by several brothers at the Phi Sigma fraternity house in East Stroudsburg.

Campus security officers have often been alerted to the presence of ghostly activities in the Auditorium of East Stroudsburg University.

Ghosts have been reported in and around The Pines, seen in this vintage post card photograph.

Indian legends abound on and near the scenic Delaware Water Gap.